FORWARD!

I first read *The Communist Manifesto* when I was about 16, and it made complete and immediate sense. Karl Marx's idea that history harbours within it vast and inexorable mechanisms that make the eventual triumph of the downtrodden masses inevitable is not only enormously empowering, it's also rather comforting. From a 16-year-old's perspective, the book is commendably short, too, while still being crammed to bursting with an all-encompassing analysis of All History Hitherto, which you can see unfolding at the bottom of this introduction.

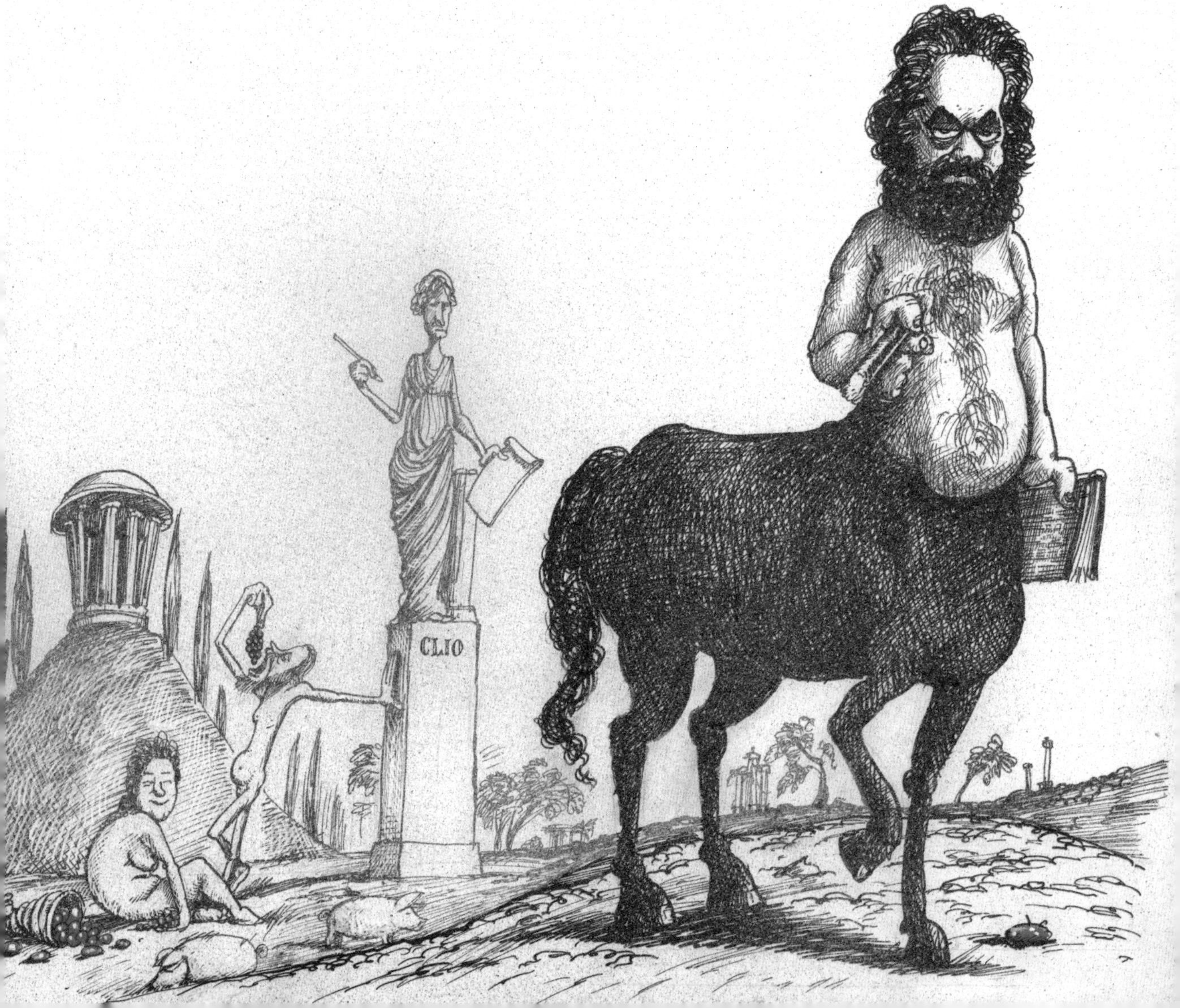
CLIO

The *Manifesto* was initially commissioned in June 1847 by the socialist group The League of the Just as a statement of its beliefs. The brief was revised at its Soho Congress that November, after its members had renamed it The Communist League. Marx finally got down to writing the *Manifesto* over a long weekend in Brussels at the end of January 1848 after the League sent him an ultimatum on 26 January demanding the text by 1 February. This is an early example of Marx's abiding brinkmanship with deadlines, which found its full flowering during the 20 years it took him to write *Das Kapital*. When he wrote *The Communist Manifesto*, with inspirational rather than concrete input from his friend, collaborator, co-author and eventual sponsor Friedrich Engels, Marx was 29 years old. Engels was 27.

Although short and written in haste, the *Manifesto* synthesised a cornucopia of ideas that had been gestating in and percolating through

Marx's thoughts for years, honed and articulated in night-long, drink-fuelled conversations with Engels. They were responding to a vast range of stimuli, from Hegel's philosophy, with its teaching about the operations of dialectics, via German Romanticism and the continuing fallout from the French Revolution, to the consequences for human beings of property, power, industrialisation and exploitation, all of it played out against the universal backdrop of history. This was the witches' brew that ended up being poured into the *Manifesto*'s 30 flimsy pages, along with a brief 10-point plan of action for government (like "Abolition of the distinction between town and country" and "Abolition of children's factory labour *in its present form*" [my italics], concluding rather vaguely with, "&c., &c."). There was also, typically of Marx, a whole section given over to rebarbative score-settling with all the rival socialists with whom he and Engels had irrevocably fallen out.

This may or may not have been what their comrades in The Communist League were expecting. Either way, when it was first published – in German, in London – the *Manifesto* hardly made any impact at all. Largely overtaken by the wave of revolutions that convulsed Europe in 1848 (but which it had done nothing to inspire or foment), in the decades of establishment reaction that followed, the *Manifesto* was forgotten. Meanwhile, Marx – in exile in London from 1851 onwards – wrote pugnacious journalism in between political committee work and failing to get on with *Das Kapital*, kept from complete penury by the timely deaths of relatives and Engels' enduring generosity, which in turn was bankrolled by Engels' job in his father's cotton mill in Manchester. Twenty years later, however, it turned out that the *Manifesto* wasn't dead after all. It was just dormant.

Interest in Marx and Engels' little pamphlet exploded following the suppression of the

Paris Commune's eight-week experiment in radical revolutionary socialism in 1871. The new French Republican Government killed more French citizens in a week crushing the Commune than Robespierre's Terror had killed in 13 months in the 1790s, while in Germany the *Manifesto* was cited as evidence for the prosecution in the trials of the leaders of the German Social Democratic Party for treason. In 1872, a new German edition was rushed out. In a new preface, Marx and Engels described the *Manifesto* as "an historical document", thus justifying their decision not to update references to, for example, Austrian Chancellor Metternich and French Prime Minister Guizot, which had been rendered redundant by both men's fall from power within days of the *Manifesto*'s initial publication in 1848. Despite this, the *Manifesto* thereafter went through dozens of editions and translations over the next 40 years. The rest, as they say, is history.

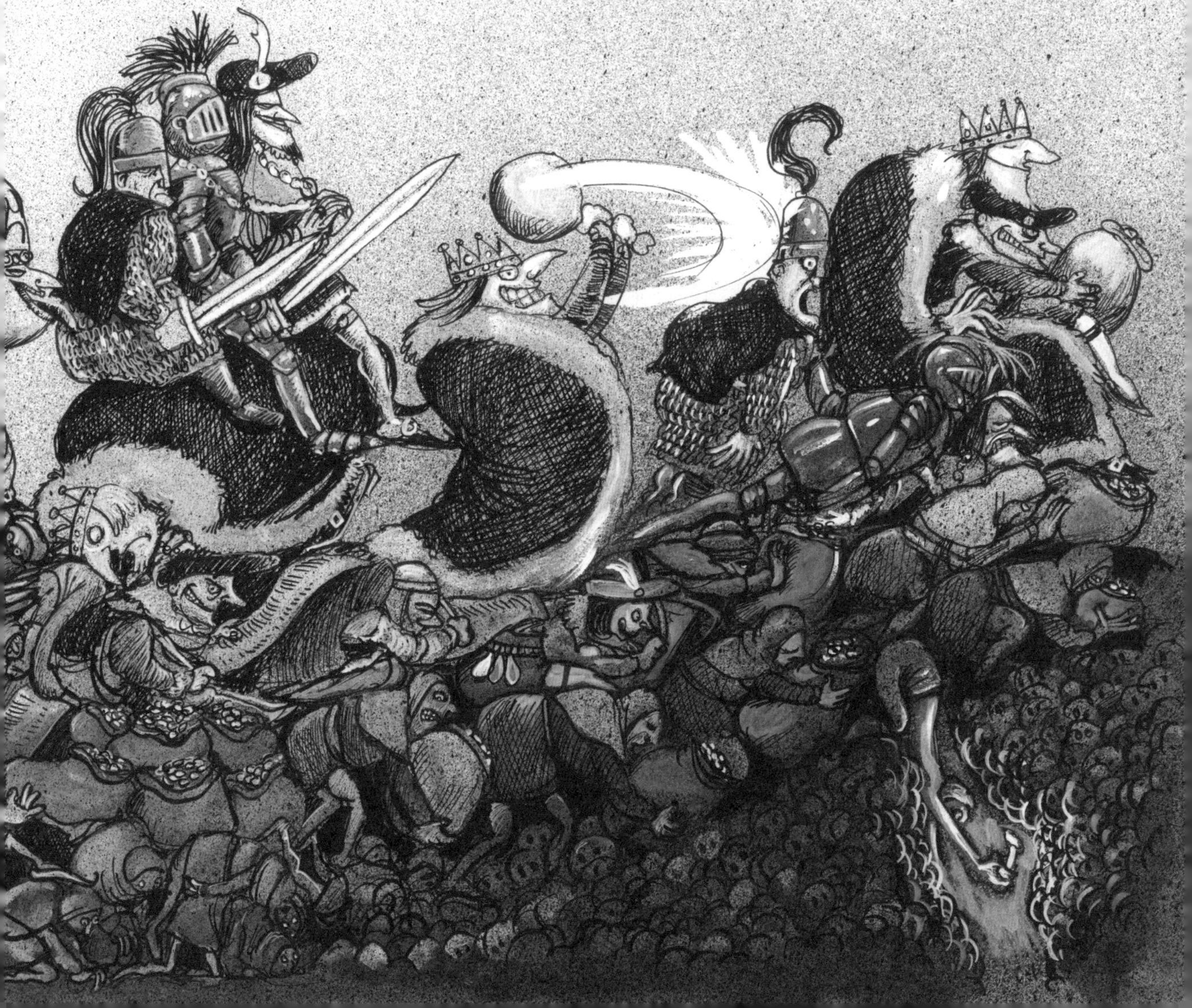

When Marx died in March 1883, Engels told the other ten mourners at the funeral that "his name and work will endure through the ages". However, I doubt that even Engels could have forecast that within a lifetime nearly half of humanity would be governed nominally according to the ideas and aspirations originally expounded in *The Communist Manifesto*, nor that in the 21st century over a fifth of us, for good or ill, would be still.

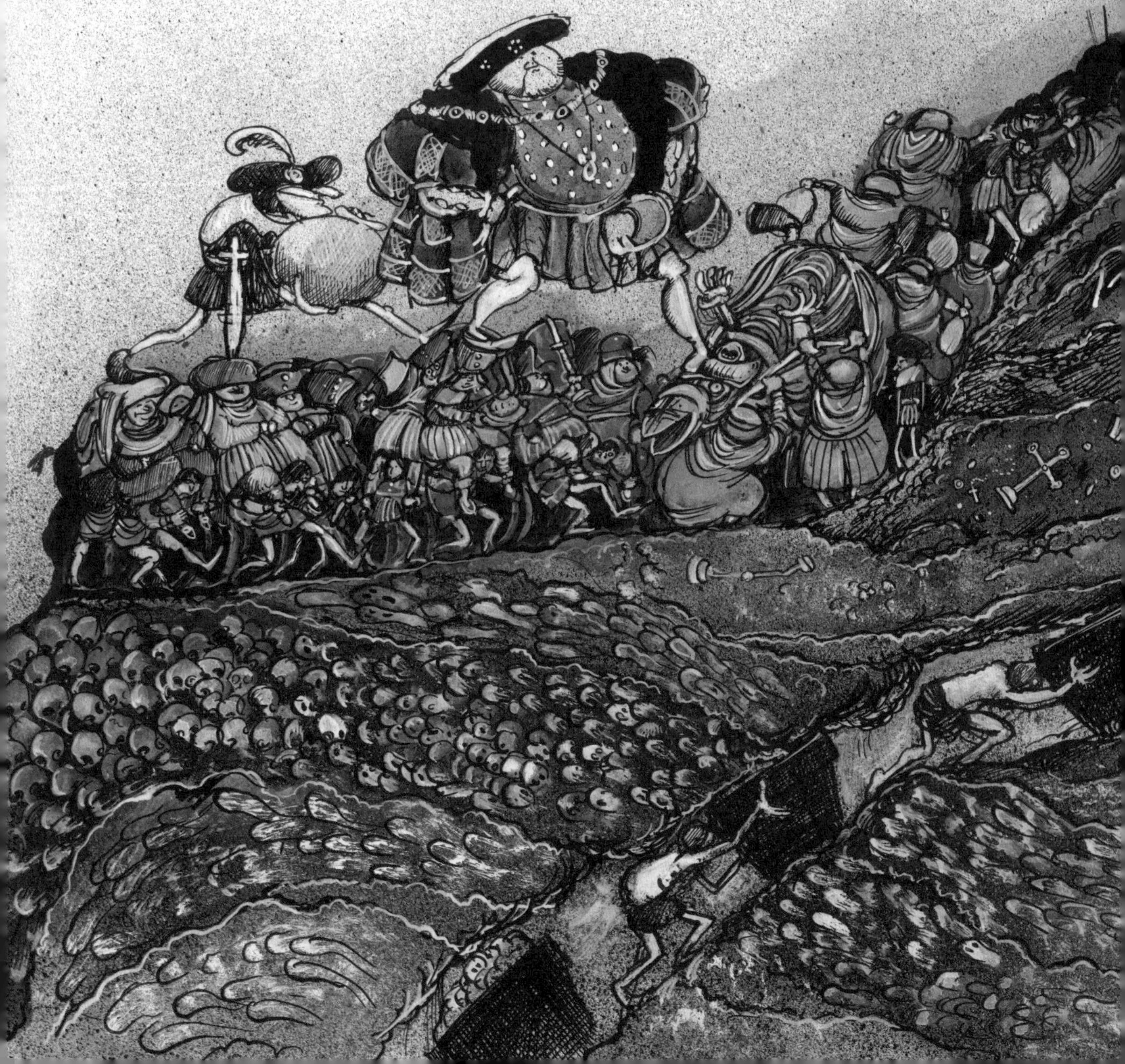

My 16-year-old self was liberated by reading *The Communist Manifesto*, although in the intervening 40 years I've come to think of Marx as being altogether too authoritarian a Hegelian sell-out merchant and too hung up on the State to be up to the essential business prescribed by his brilliant analyses. These include his materialist version of history and his vision of human beings reduced through exploitation and appropriation (what we'd call theft) to mere

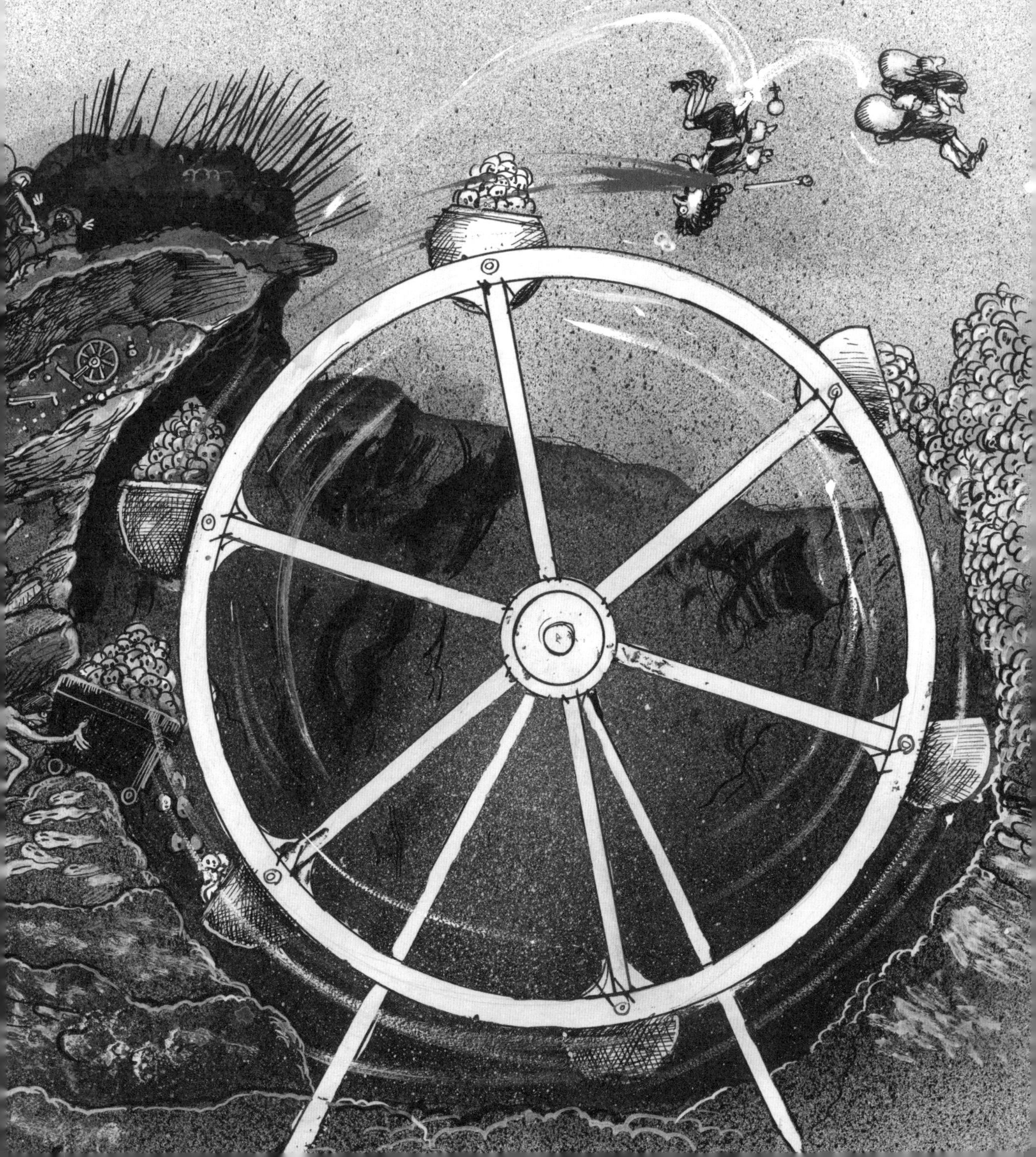

commodities, just meat machines existing solely to be milked for their surplus value, further to enrich the already rich. I also still relish the irony that this compelling reading of history and human affairs as being almost geological in their tectonic clash of classes, and thus being wholly impersonal, was promulgated by a couple of blokes down the pub who thereby changed the world. In fact, Marx and Engels were no strangers to pubs. During his long London exile,

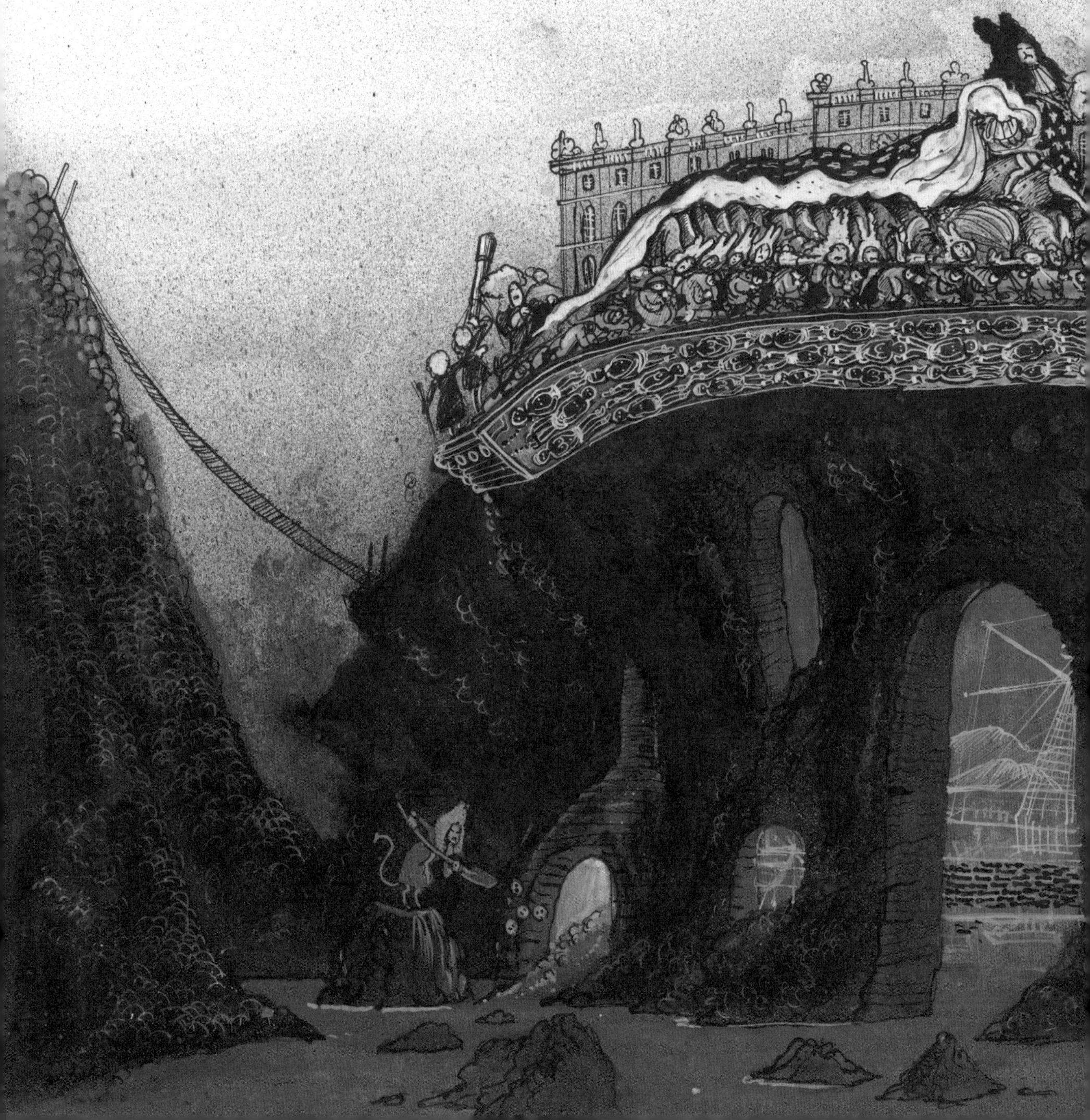

Marx often propped up the bar of The Pindar of Wakefield in King's Cross. Later barflies in the same pub, now renamed The Water Rats, have included Lenin, Bob Dylan, The Pogues and Oasis, the last three of whom all played their first London gigs there. But I fear even the keenest Marxist historian might falter in attempting to tease out a wider historical significance connecting Karl Marx and both Shane MacGowan and Noel Gallagher.

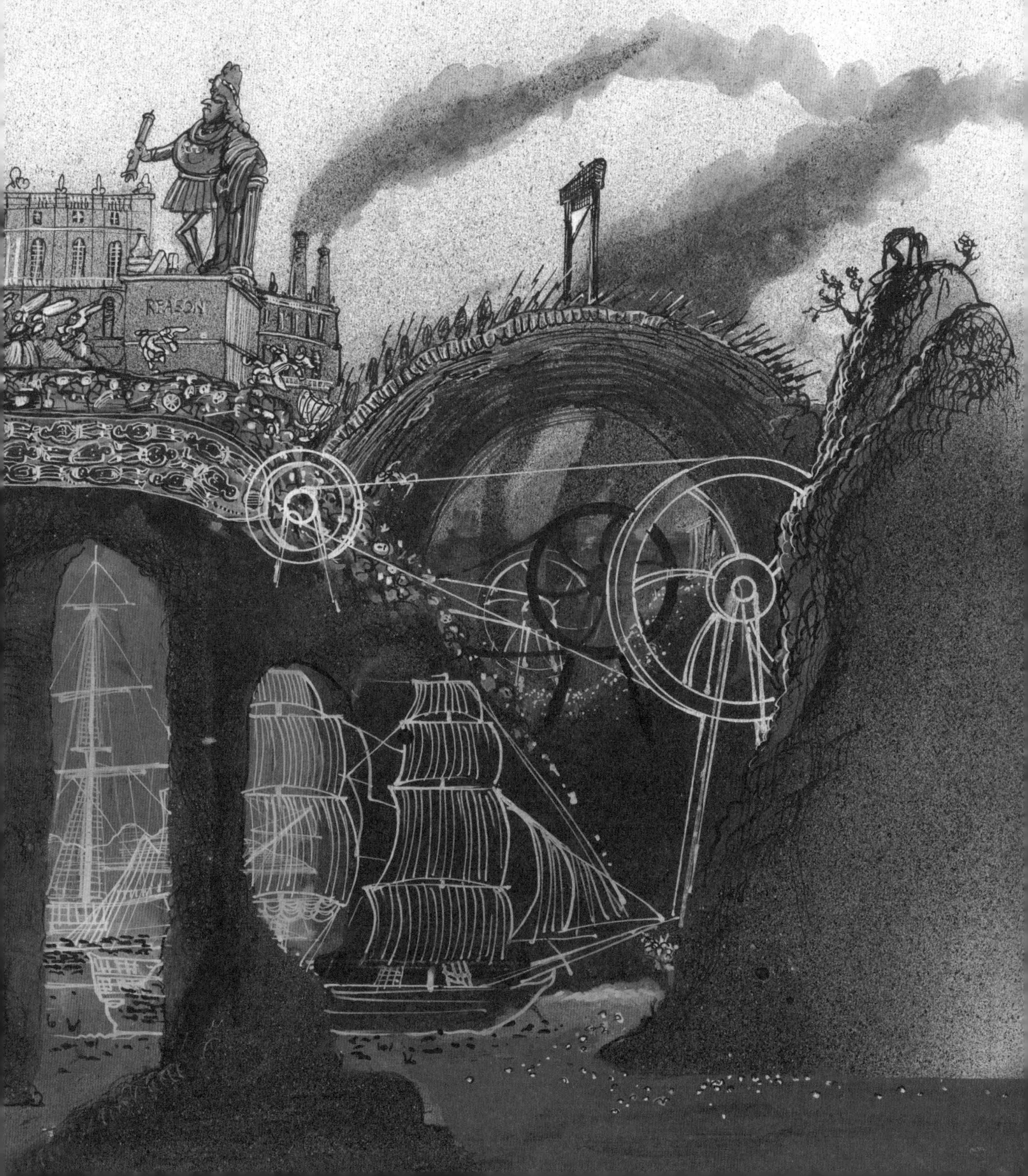
REASON

As we know, history – thus far, at least – has failed to unfold precisely as Marx either hoped or prophesied, though it's not Marx's fault that in most revolutions the battering ram aimed against the walls of the elite always seems to buckle at the last minute, ending up buttressing the even higher walls of new elites, themselves now fuelled by a thirst for revenge.

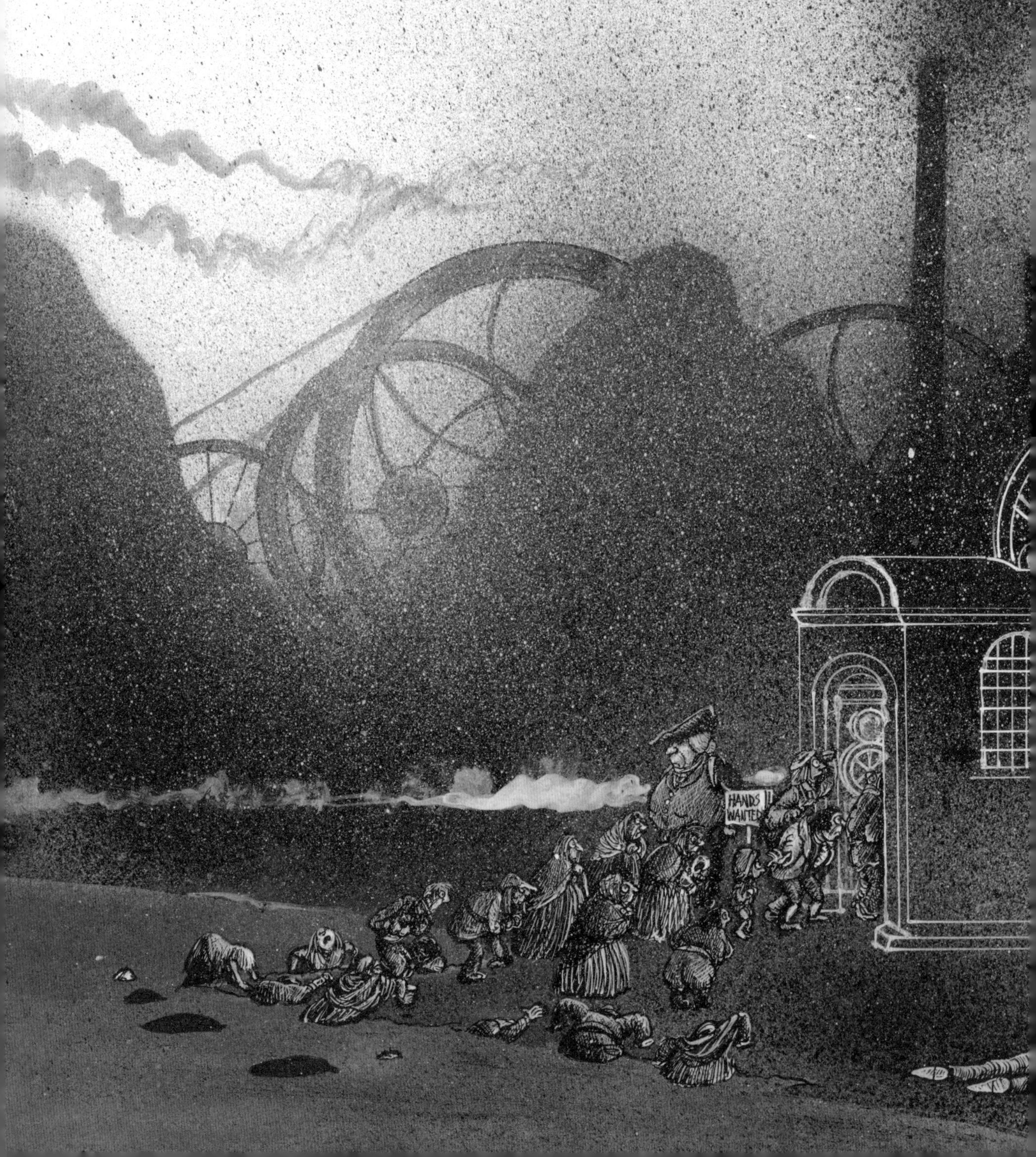
HANDS WANTED

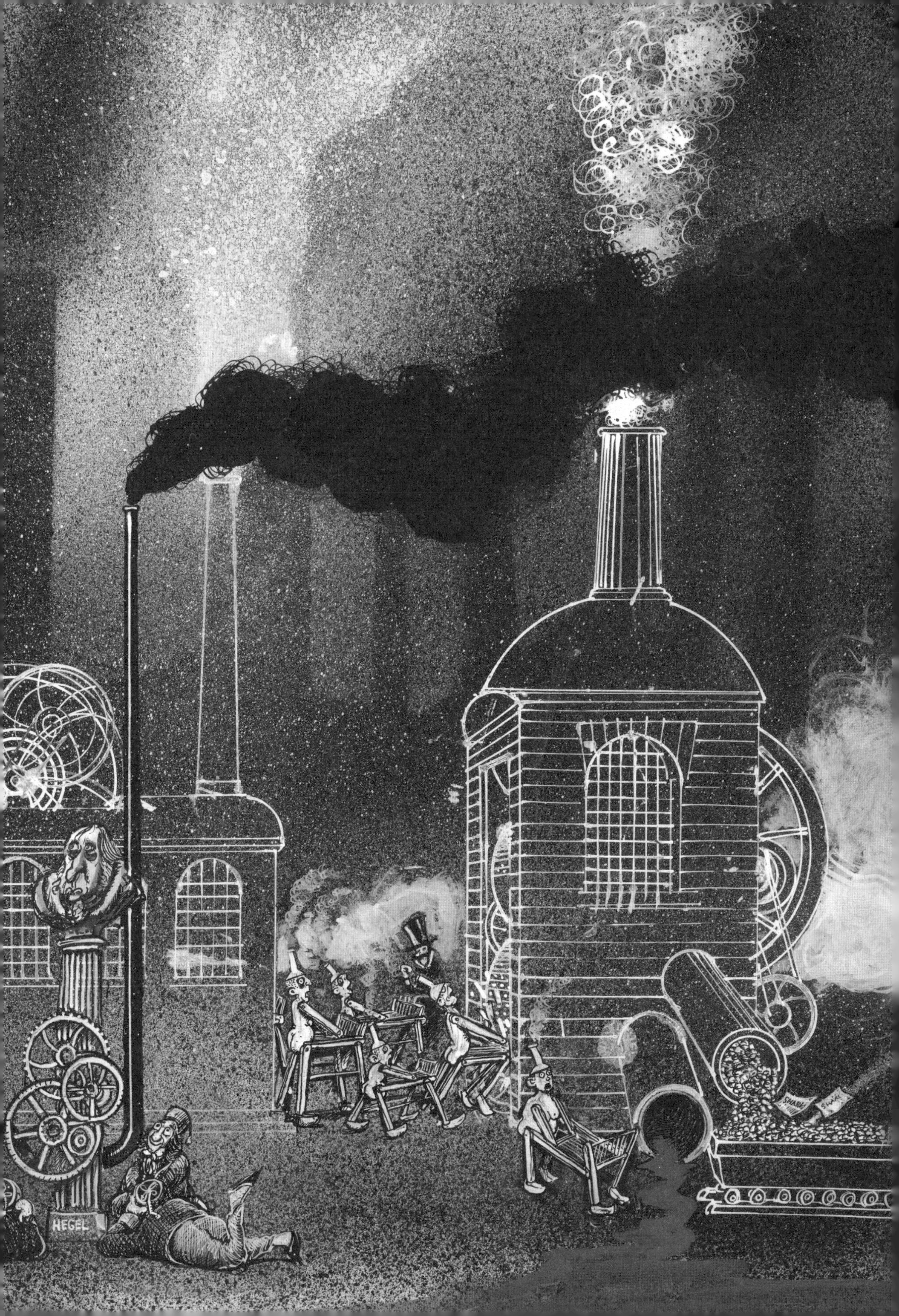
HEGEL

Nor, for that matter, are Marxists entirely Marx's fault, either. In all their mutually hostile and frequently murderous variety, on top of the romantic revolutionaries, freedom fighters, heroes and heroines, academics, despots, death cultists or boneheaded bureaucrats, and ignoring the President of North Korea and the Central Committee of the Chinese Communist Party, the Marxist diaspora encompasses everyone from former Trot Ayn Randists and neo-cons

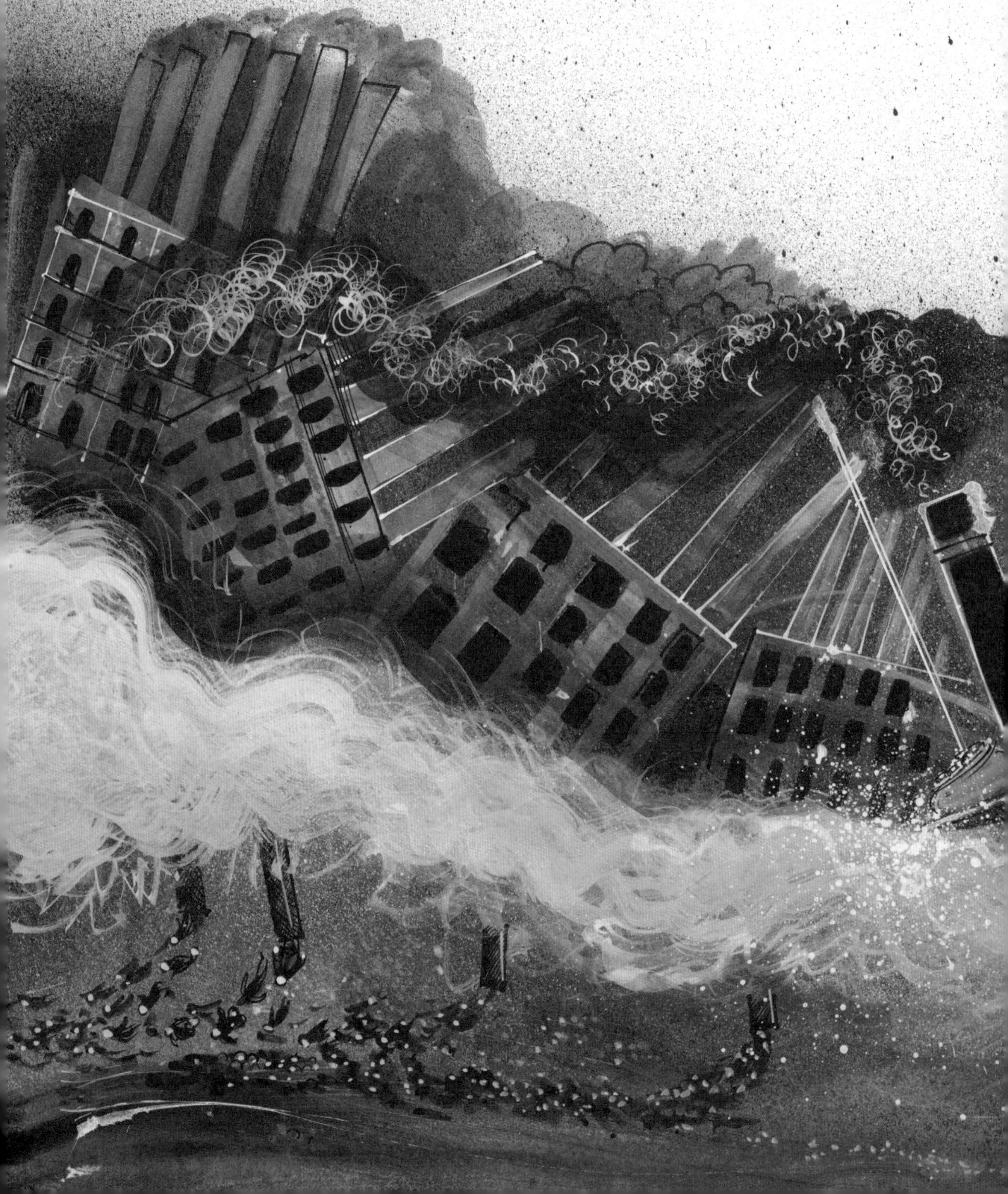

and ex-tankie habitués of the salons of New Labour to things as worryingly weird as Peter Hitchens, Sp!ked Online and wizened old Maoists maintaining sequestered harems of adoring female comrades in Neasden. I imagine absolutely all of them will hate this book.

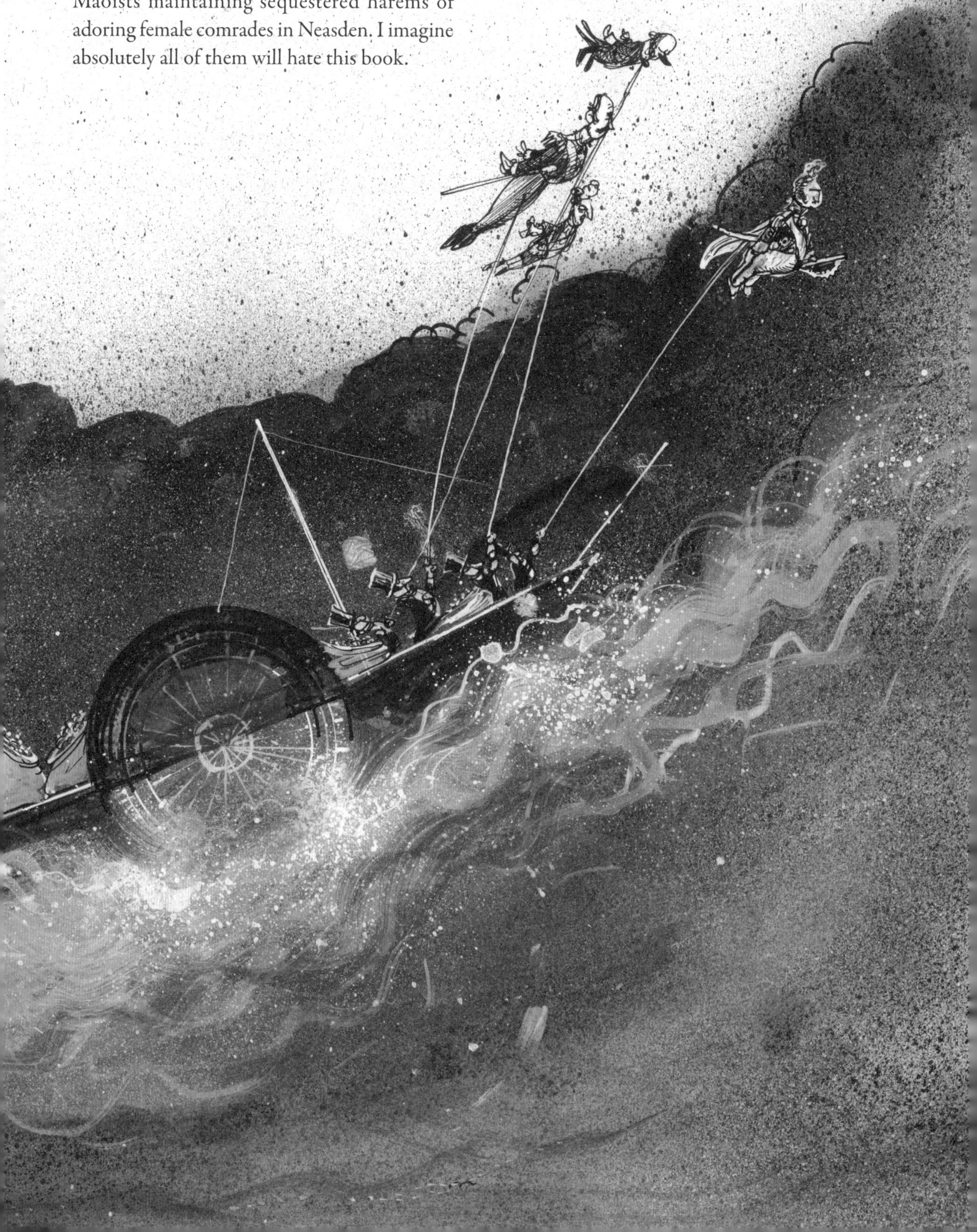

Marx, I hope, would like it. I hope it's true to a wider, deeper Marx, who as a student was so obsessed with Laurence Sterne's *The Life and Opinions of Tristram Shandy* that he wrote *Scorpion and Felix* – 300 pages of what his biographer Francis Wheen describes as "whimsy and persiflage" – in awed imitation.

Moreover, 170 years after writing *The Communist Manifesto*, when just 43 individuals possess as much wealth as half of the rest of our entire species, Marx still has a lot left to say. I hope the following helps him say it.

Martin Rowson
January 2018
Lewisham

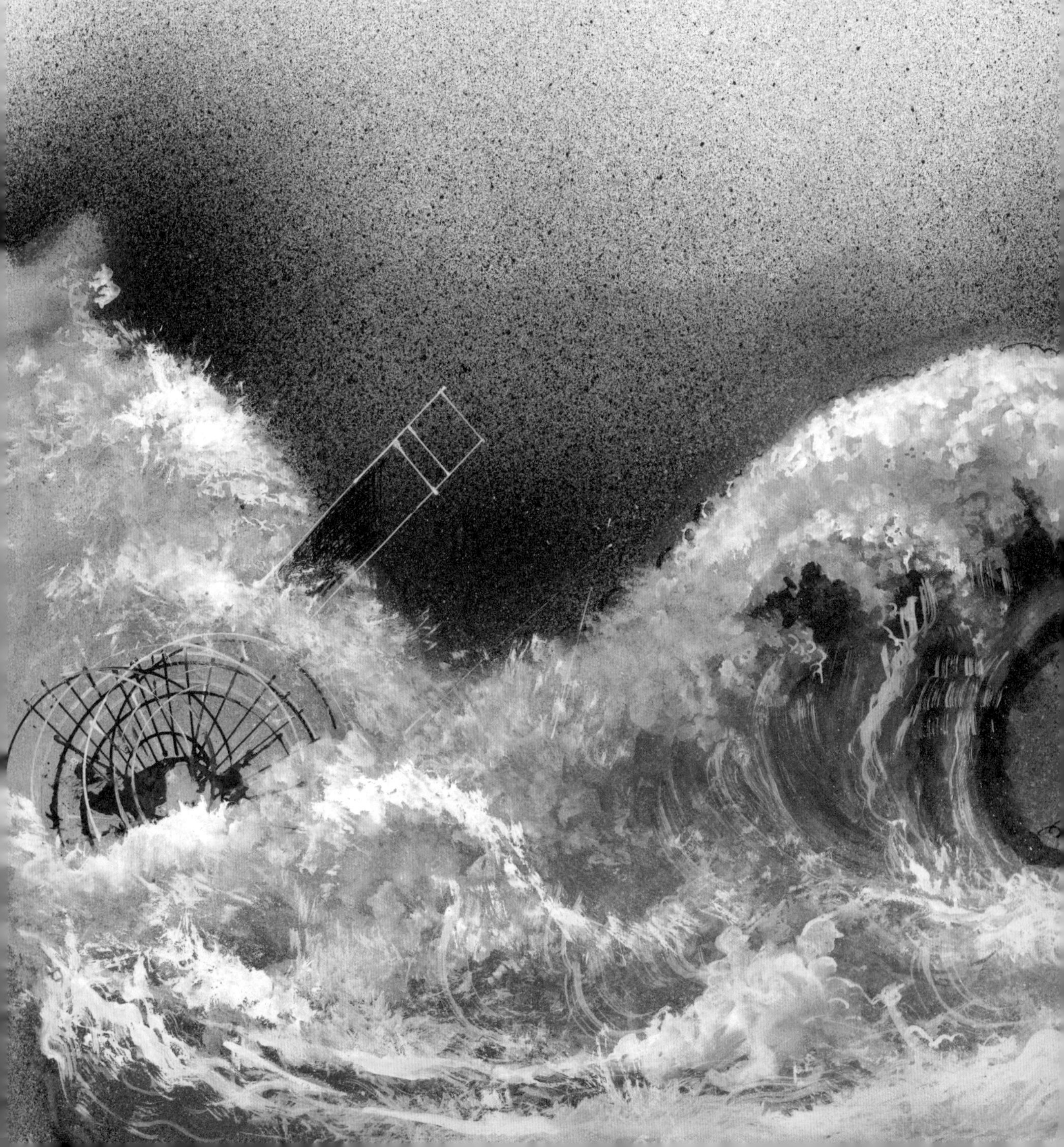

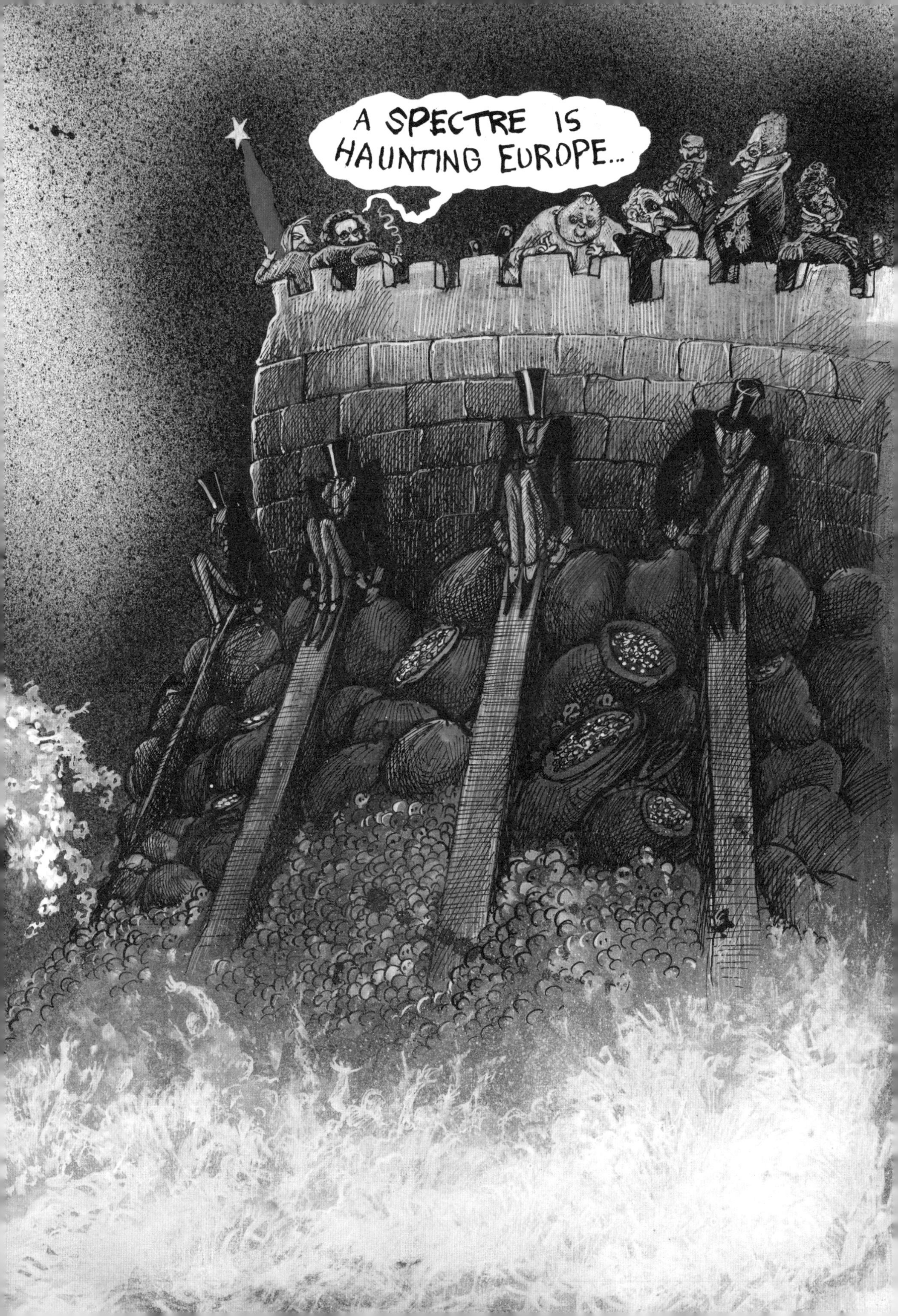
A SPECTRE IS HAUNTING EUROPE...

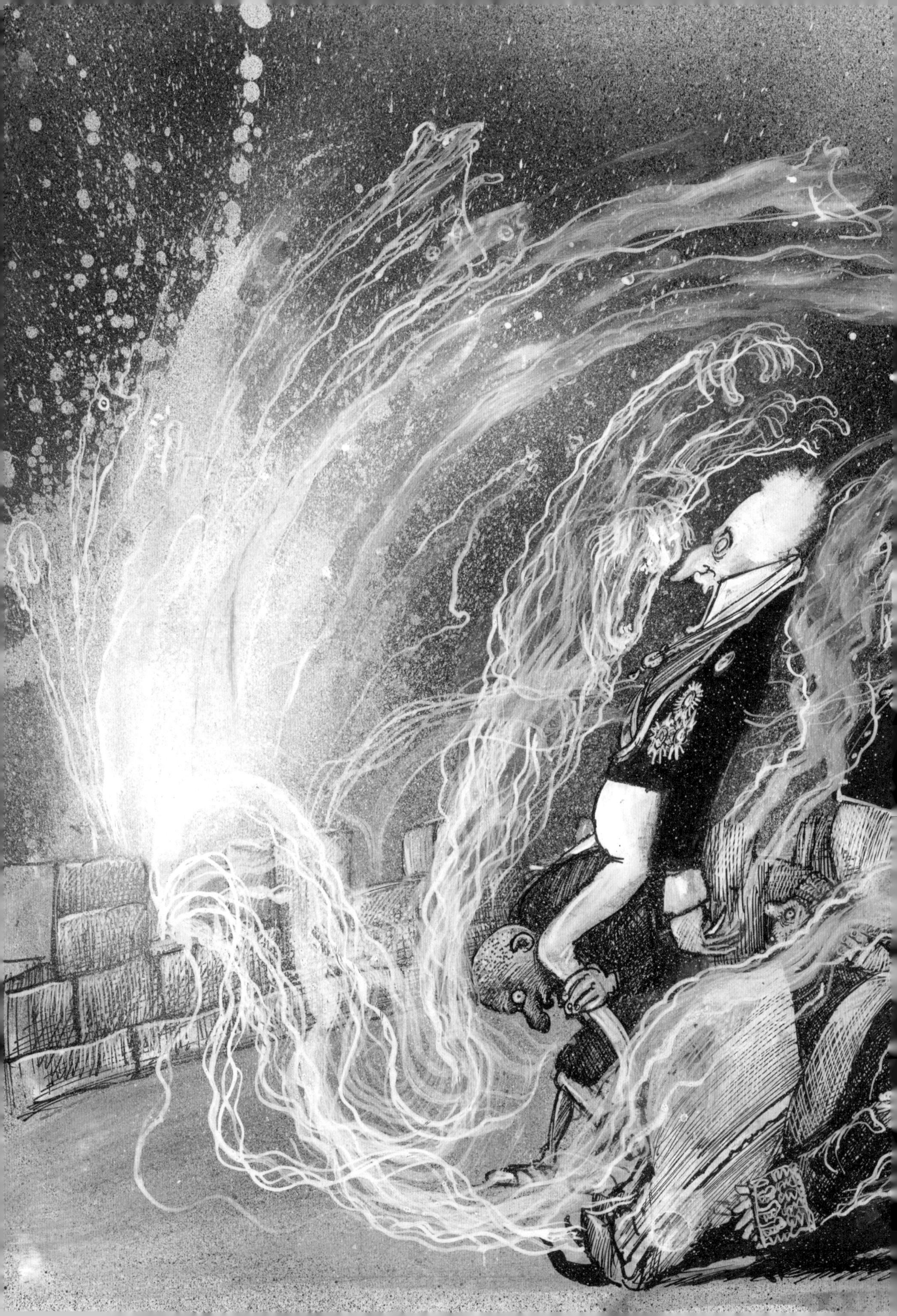

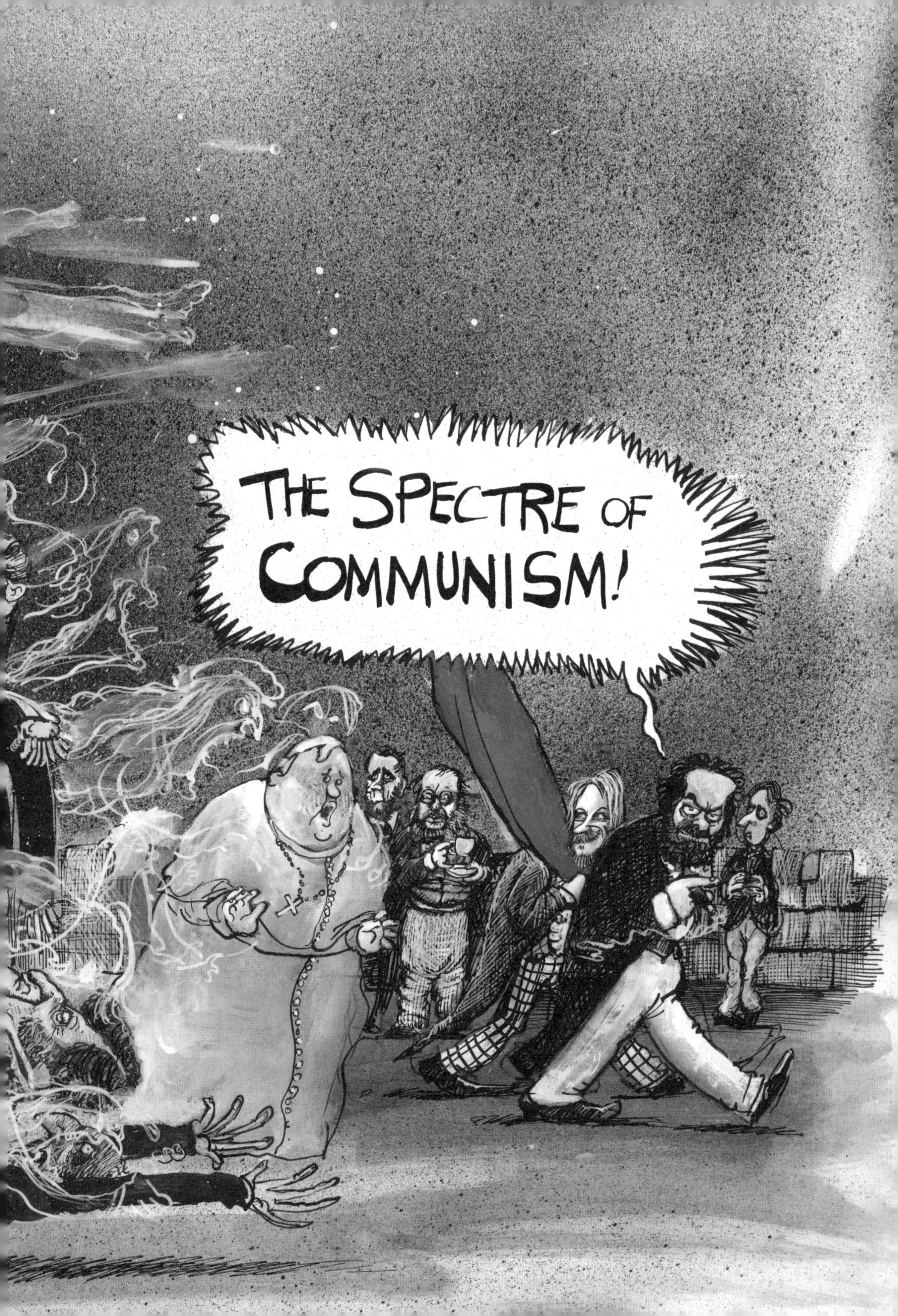
THE SPECTRE OF COMMUNISM!

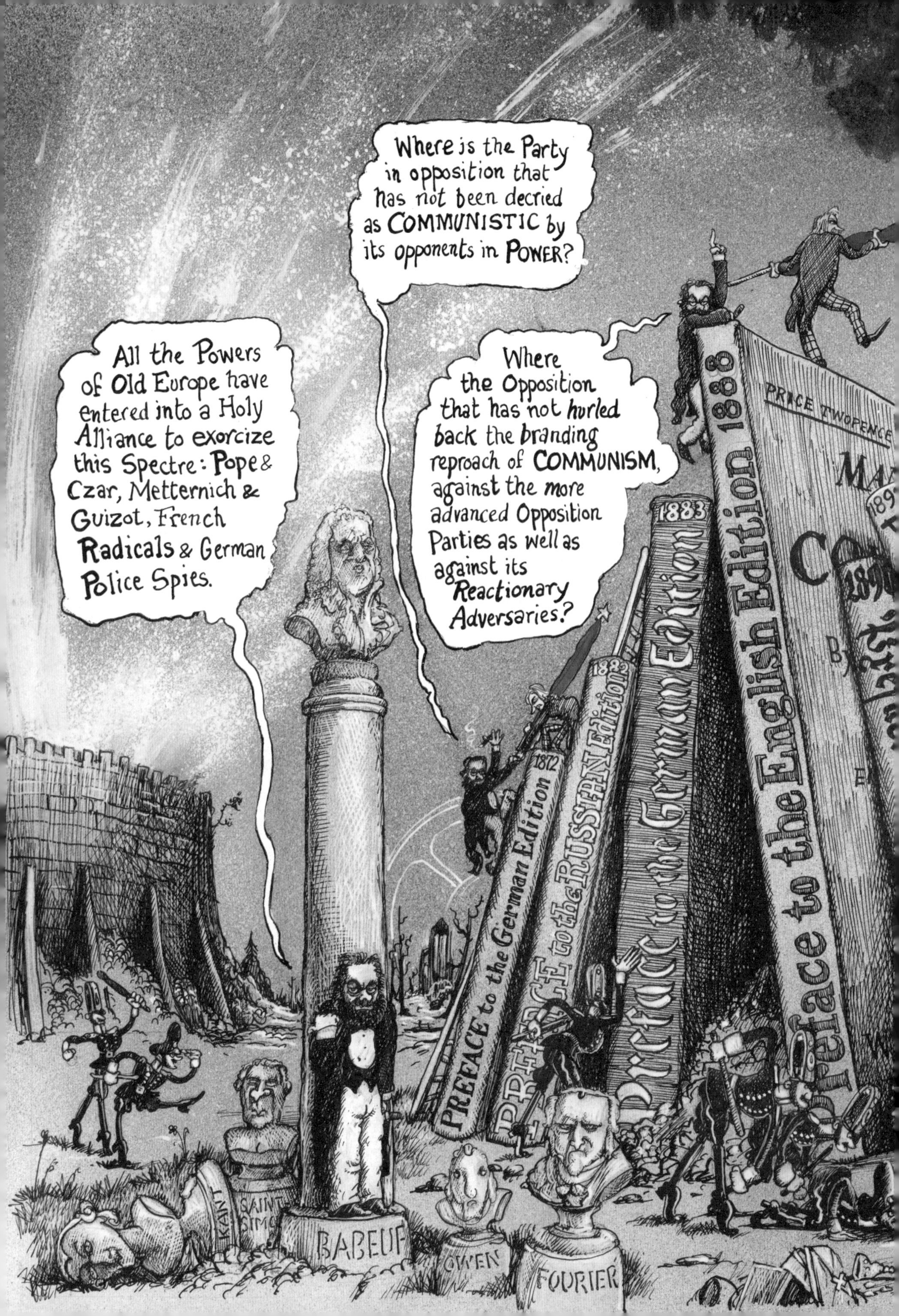
All the Powers of Old Europe have entered into a Holy Alliance to exorcize this Spectre: Pope & Czar, Metternich & Guizot, French Radicals & German Police Spies.
Where is the Party in opposition that has not been decried as COMMUNISTIC by its opponents in POWER?
Where the Opposition that has not hurled back the branding reproach of COMMUNISM, against the more advanced Opposition Parties as well as against its Reactionary Adversaries?
1872
PREFACE to the German Edition
1882
PREFACE to the RUSSIAN Edition
1883
Preface to the German Edition
1888
Preface to the English Edition
PRICE TWOPENCE
KANT
BABEUF
OWEN
FOURIER

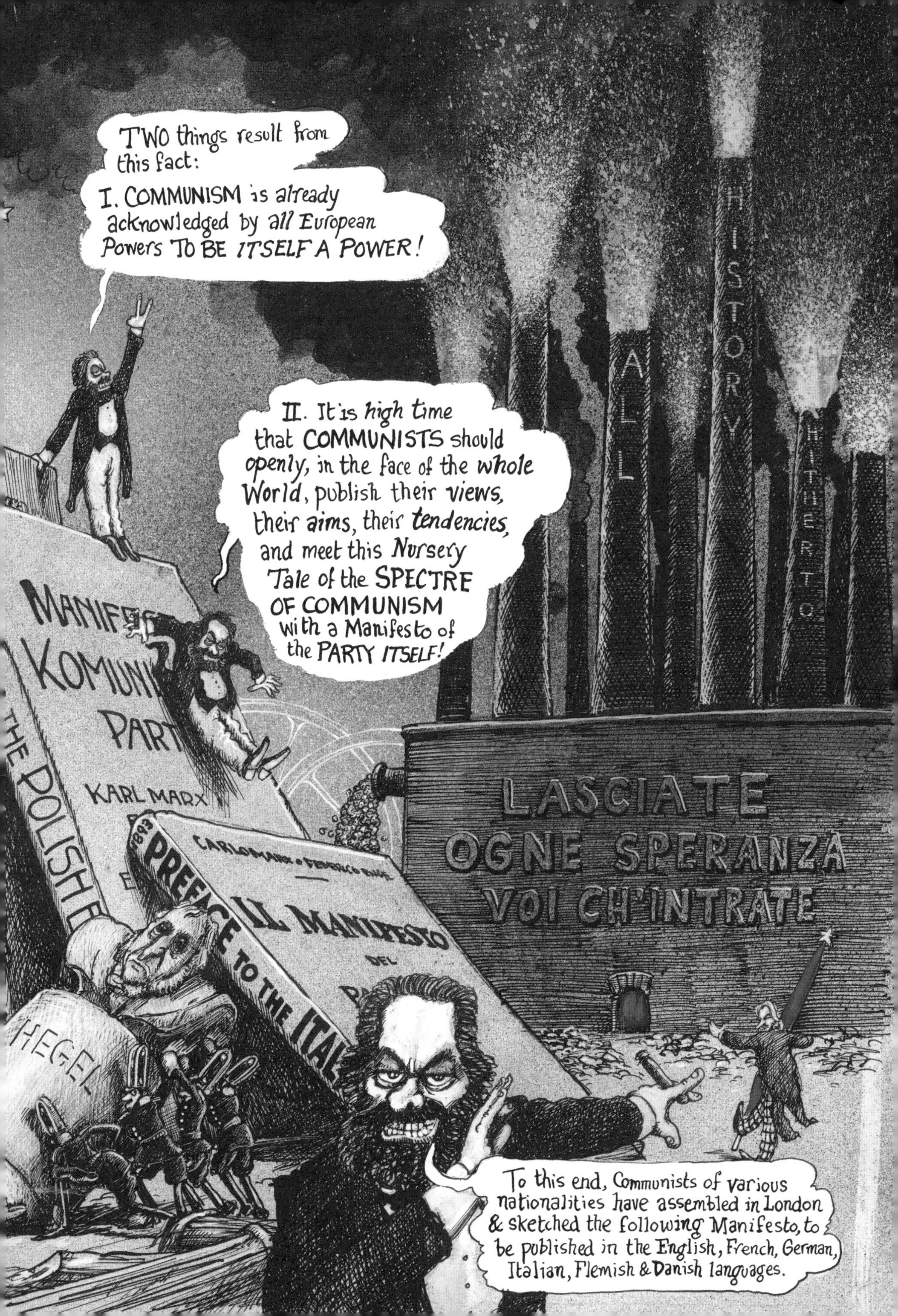
TWO things result from this fact:
I. COMMUNISM is already acknowledged by all European Powers TO BE ITSELF A POWER!
II. It is high time that COMMUNISTS should openly, in the face of the whole World, publish their views, their aims, their tendencies, and meet this Nursery Tale of the SPECTRE OF COMMUNISM with a Manifesto of the PARTY ITSELF!
ALL HISTORY HITHERTO
KARL MARX
1893
IL MANIFESTO
HEGEL
LASCIATE OGNE SPERANZA VOI CH'INTRATE
To this end, Communists of various nationalities have assembled in London & sketched the following Manifesto, to be published in the English, French, German, Italian, Flemish & Danish languages.

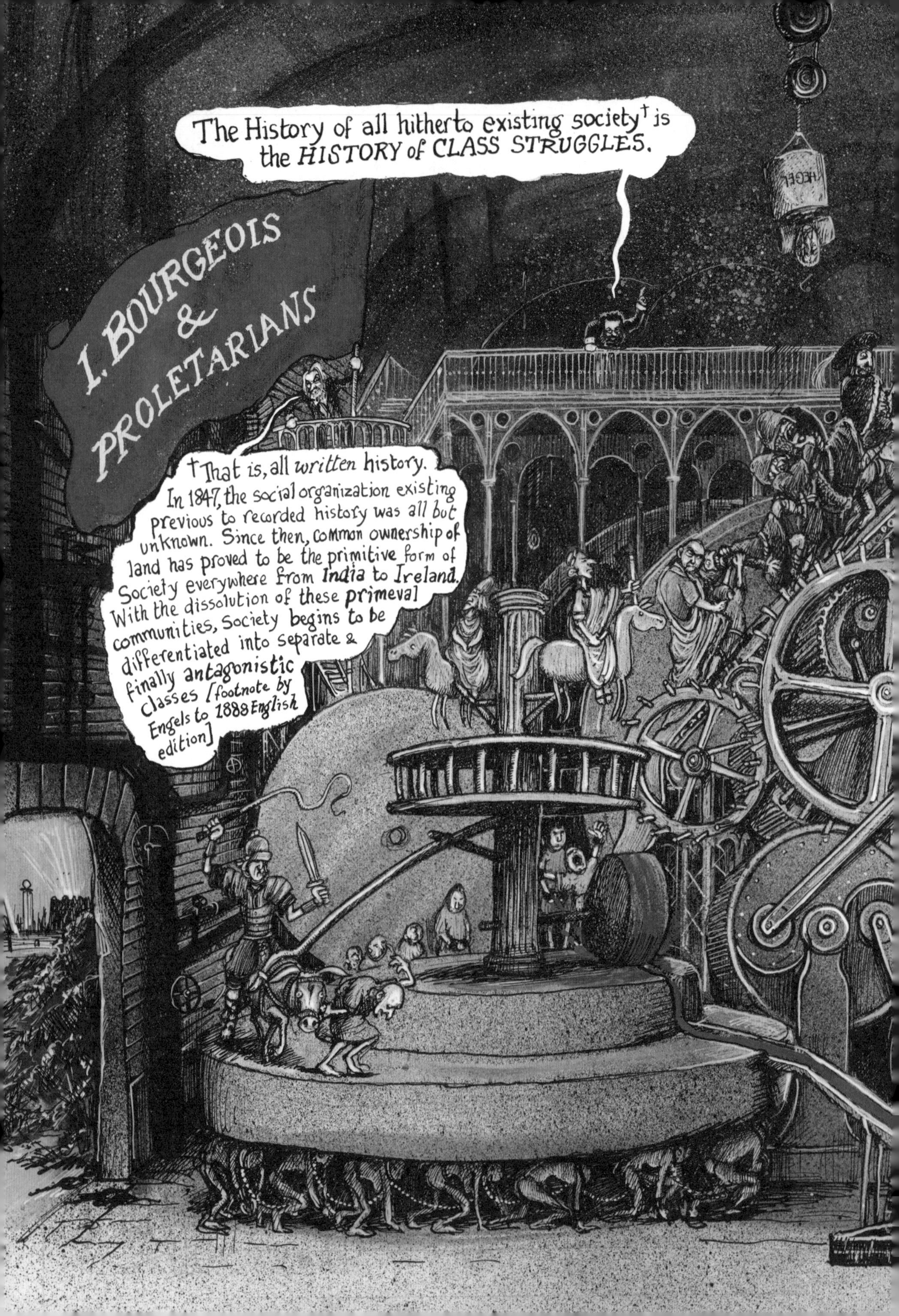
The History of all hitherto existing society† is the HISTORY of CLASS STRUGGLES.
I. BOURGEOIS & PROLETARIANS
†That is, all written history. In 1847, the social organization existing previous to recorded history was all but unknown. Since then, common ownership of land has proved to be the primitive form of Society everywhere from India to Ireland. With the dissolution of these primeval communities, Society begins to be differentiated into separate & finally antagonistic classes [footnote by Engels to 1888 English edition]

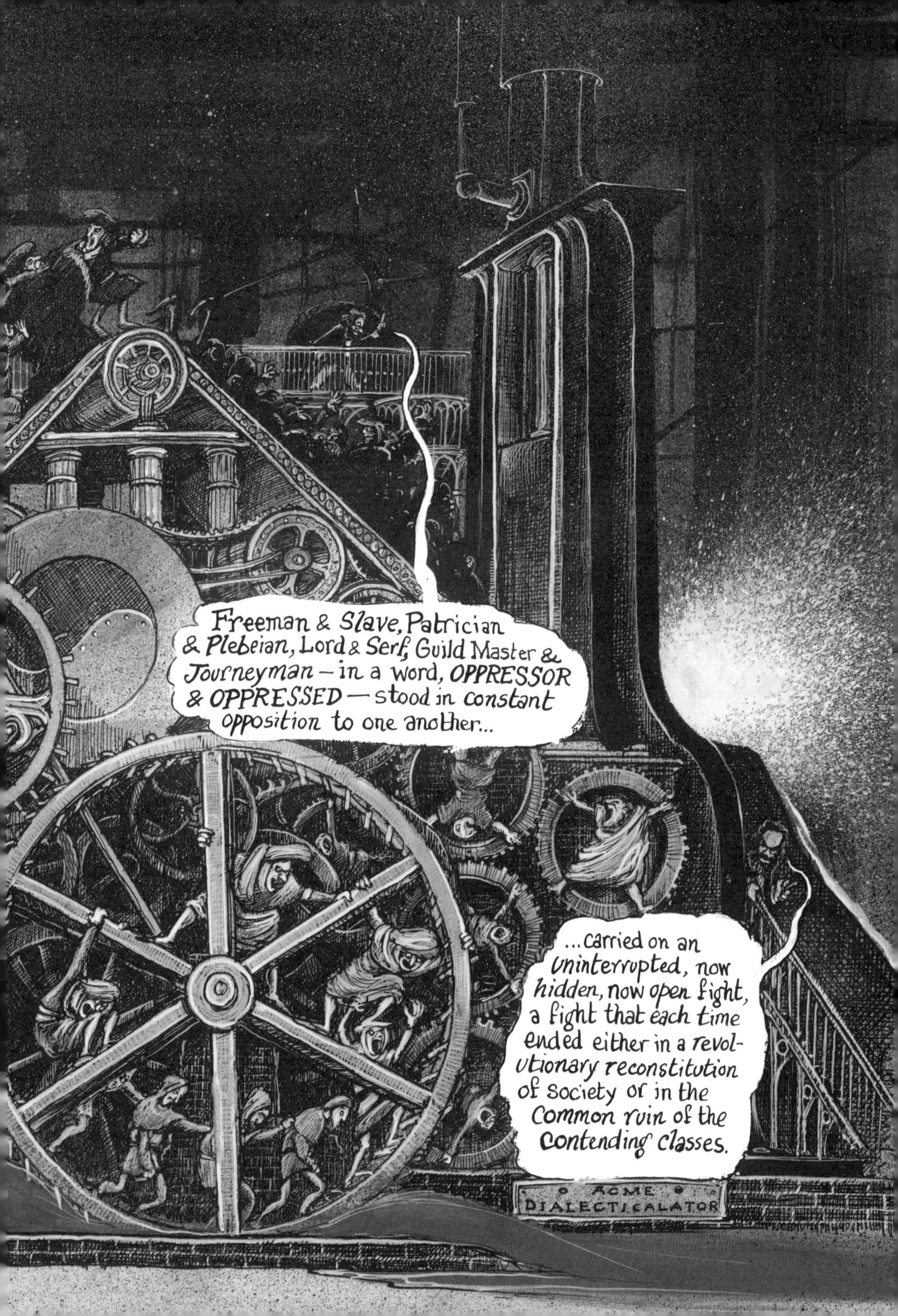
Freeman & Slave, Patrician & Plebeian, Lord & Serf, Guild Master & Journeyman – in a word, OPPRESSOR & OPPRESSED – stood in constant opposition to one another...
...carried on an uninterrupted, now hidden, now open fight, a fight that each time ended either in a revolutionary reconstitution of society or in the common ruin of the contending classes.
ACME DIALECTICALATOR

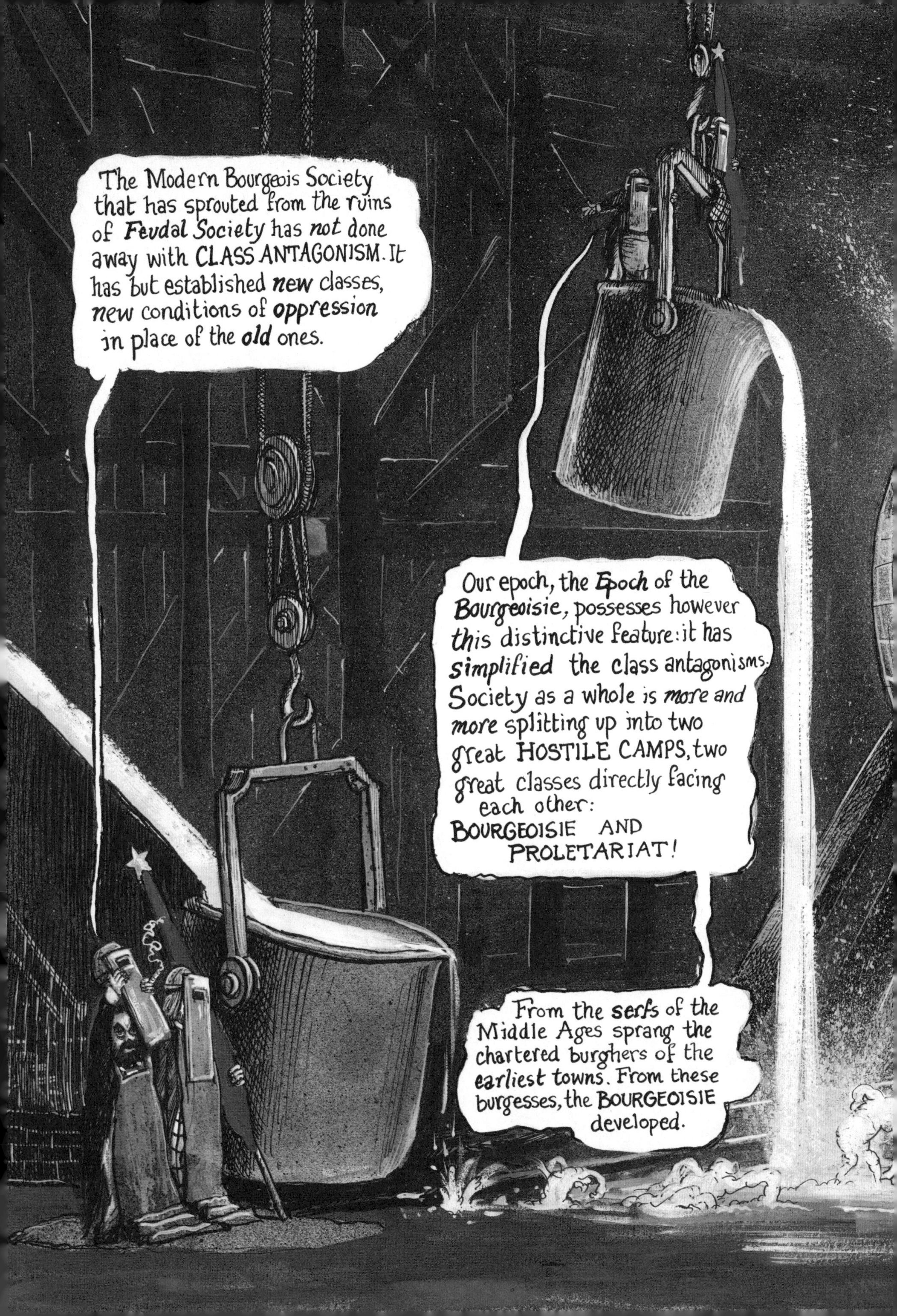
The Modern Bourgeois Society that has sprouted from the ruins of Feudal Society has not done away with CLASS ANTAGONISM. It has but established new classes, new conditions of oppression in place of the old ones.
Our epoch, the Epoch of the Bourgeoisie, possesses however this distinctive feature: it has simplified the class antagonisms. Society as a whole is more and more splitting up into two great HOSTILE CAMPS, two great classes directly facing each other: BOURGEOISIE AND PROLETARIAT!
From the serfs of the Middle Ages sprang the chartered burghers of the earliest towns. From these burgesses, the BOURGEOISIE developed.

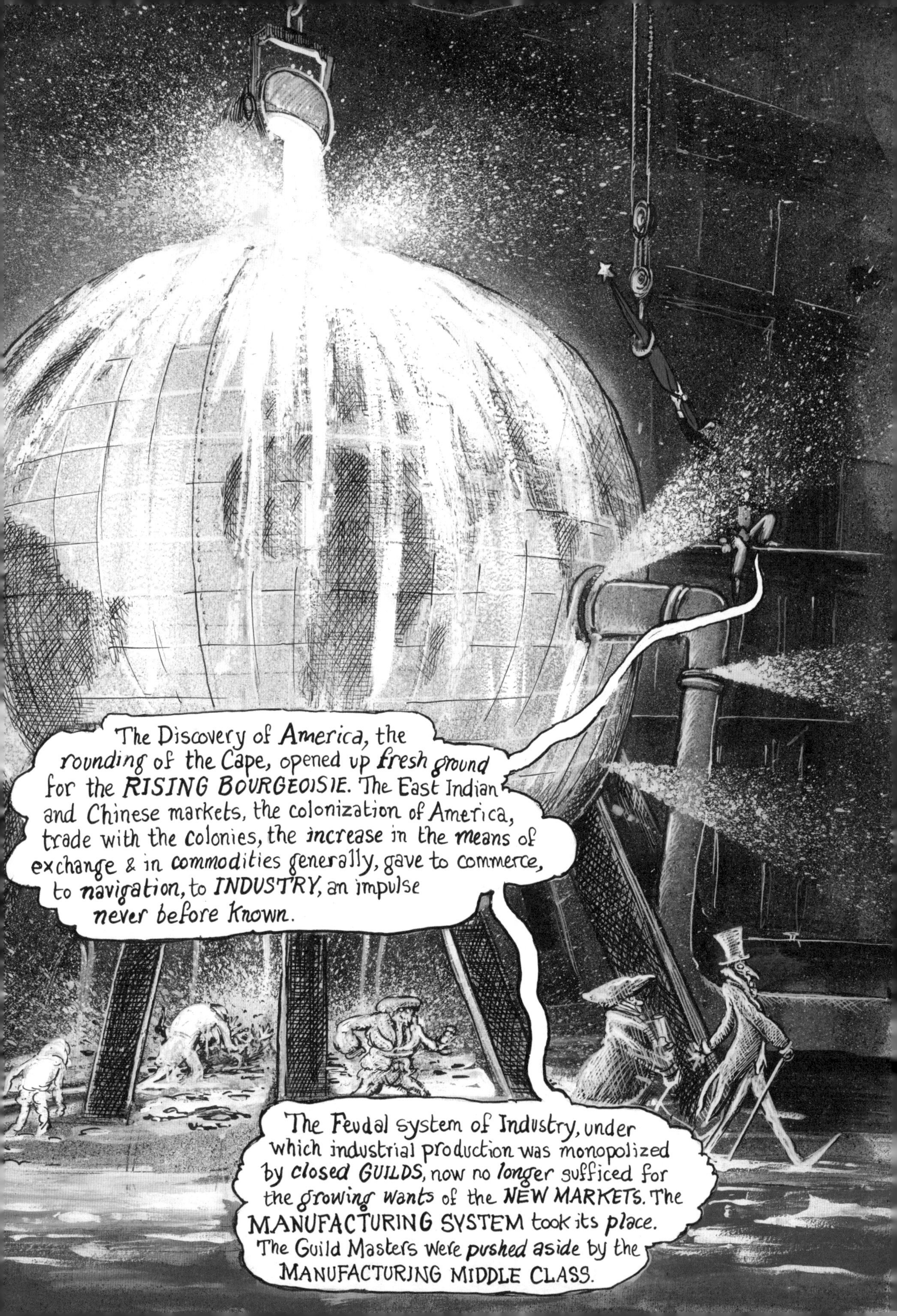

The Discovery of America, the rounding of the Cape, opened up fresh ground for the RISING BOURGEOISIE. The East Indian and Chinese markets, the colonization of America, trade with the colonies, the increase in the means of exchange & in commodities generally, gave to commerce, to navigation, to INDUSTRY, an impulse never before known.
The Feudal system of Industry, under which industrial production was monopolized by closed GUILDS, now no longer sufficed for the growing wants of the NEW MARKETS. The MANUFACTURING SYSTEM took its place. The Guild Masters were pushed aside by the MANUFACTURING MIDDLE CLASS.

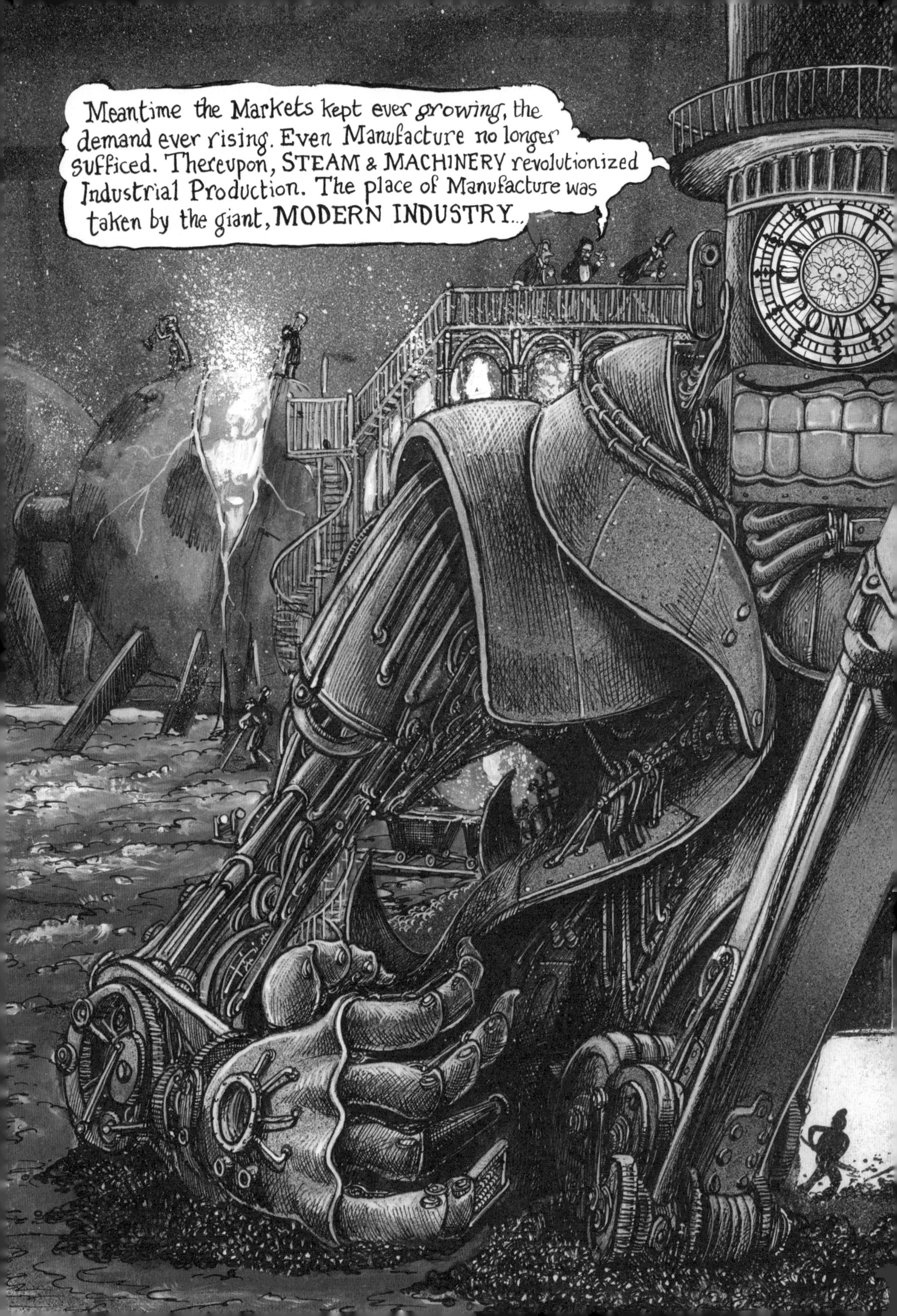
Meantime the Markets kept ever *growing*, the demand ever rising. Even Manufacture no longer sufficed. Thereupon, STEAM & MACHINERY revolutionized Industrial Production. The place of Manufacture was taken by the giant, MODERN INDUSTRY...
CAPITA
POWER

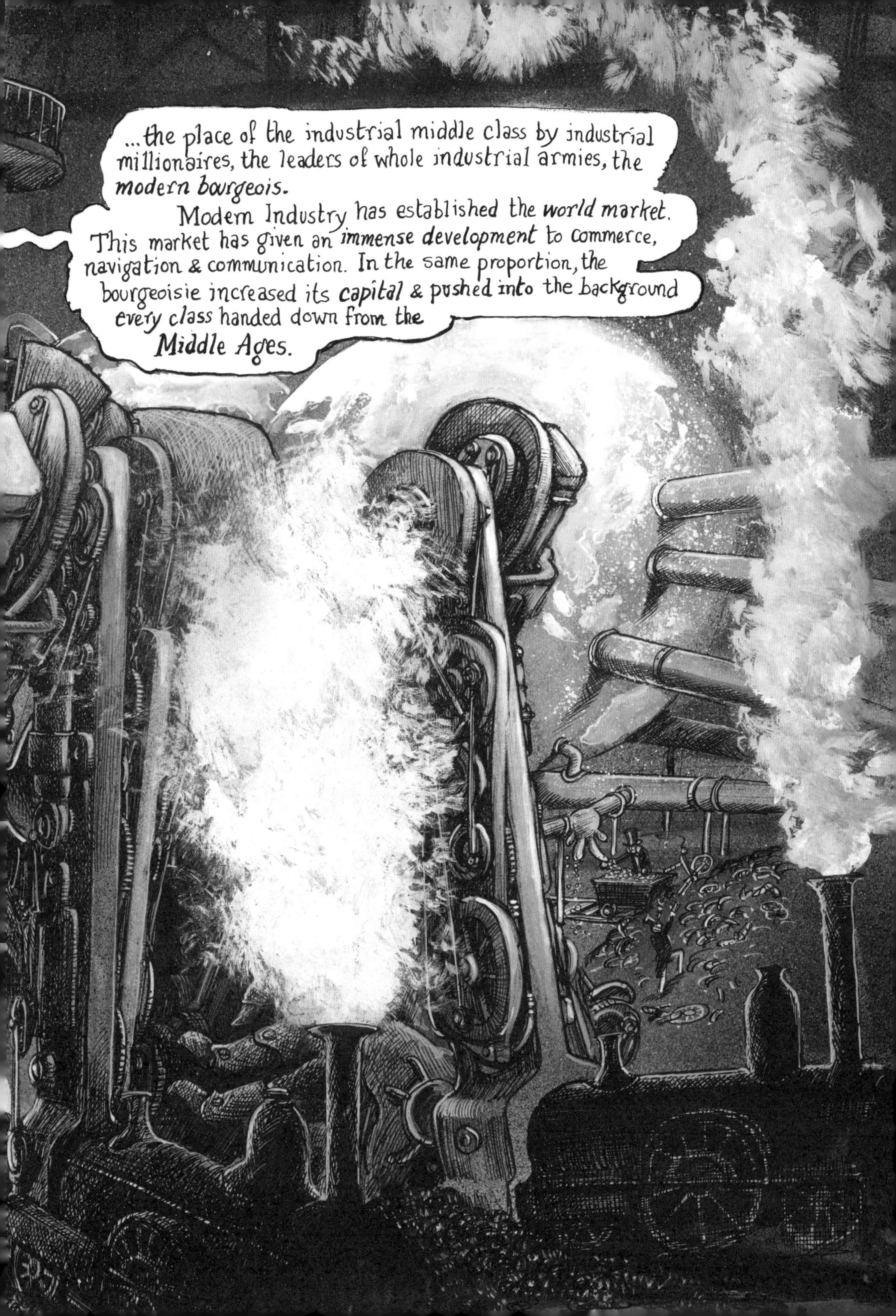
...the place of the industrial middle class by industrial millionaires, the leaders of whole industrial armies, the modern bourgeois. Modern Industry has established the world market. This market has given an immense development to commerce, navigation & communication. In the same proportion, the bourgeoisie increased its capital & pushed into the background every class handed down from the Middle Ages.

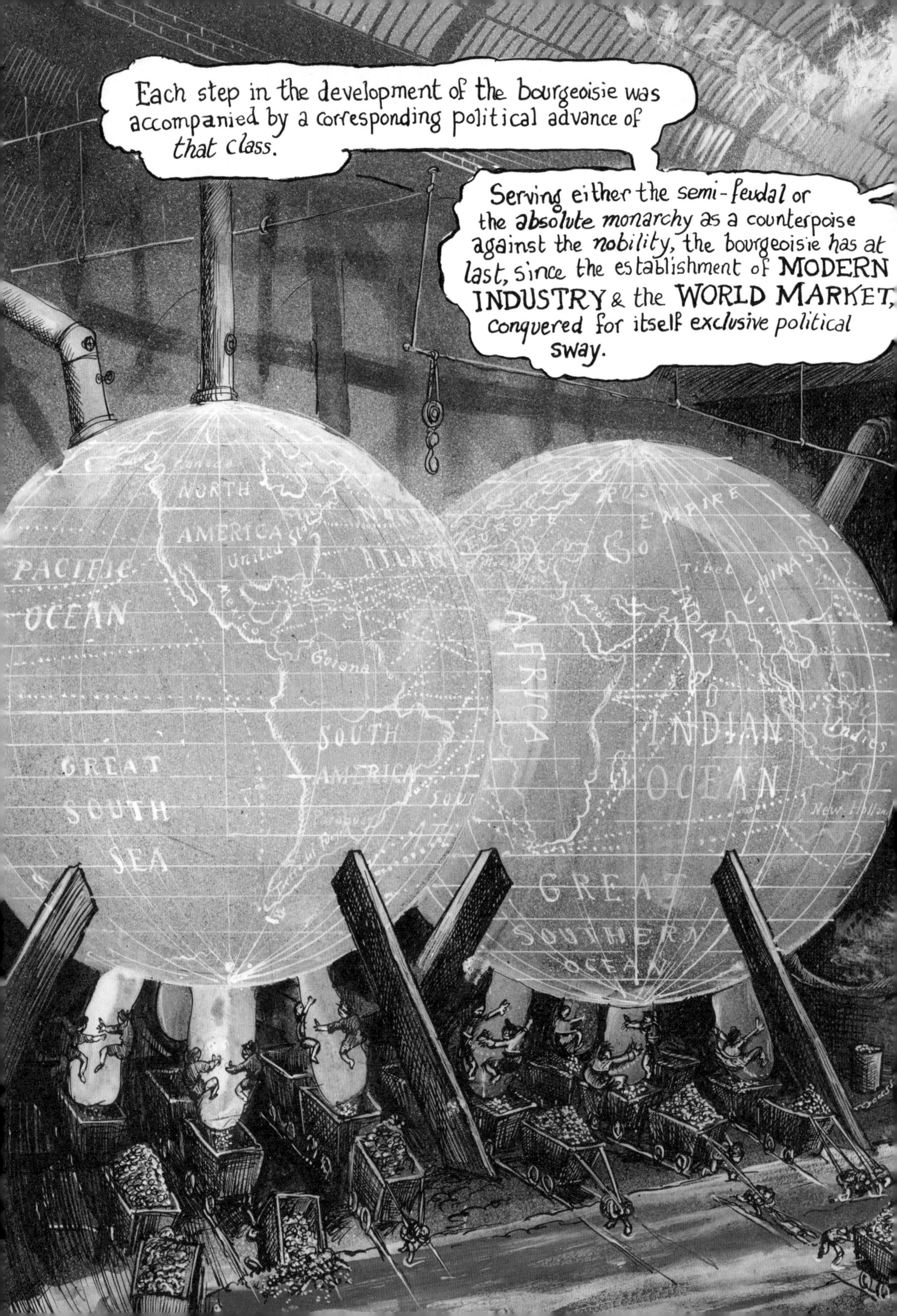

Each step in the development of the bourgeoisie was accompanied by a corresponding political advance of *that* class.
Serving either the semi-feudal or the *absolute monarchy* as a counterpoise against the *nobility*, the bourgeoisie has at last, since the establishment of MODERN INDUSTRY & the WORLD MARKET, conquered for itself exclusive political sway.
NORTH AMERICA
PACIFIC OCEAN
SOUTH AMERICA
GREAT SOUTH SEA
AFRICA
INDIAN OCEAN
GREAT SOUTHERN OCEAN

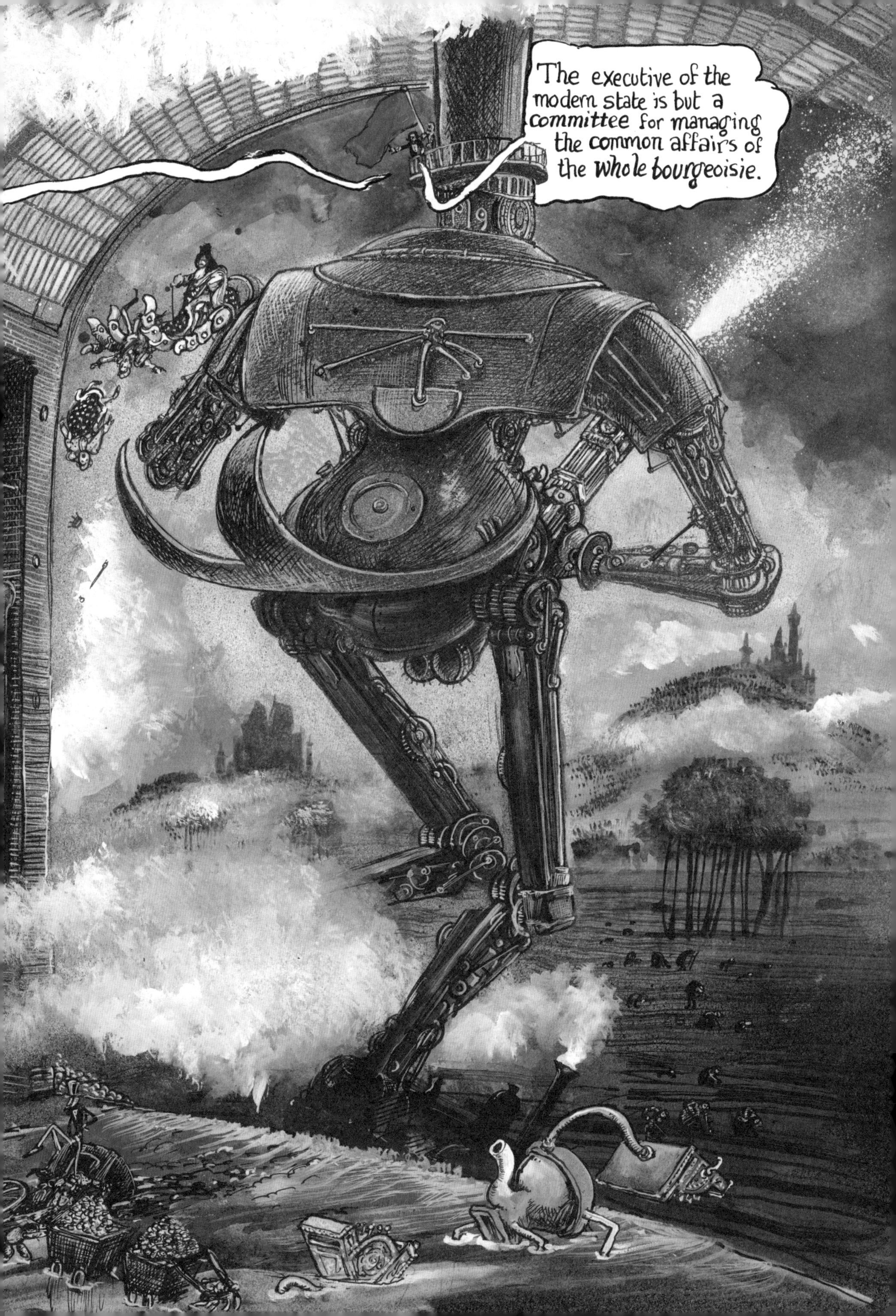
The executive of the modern state is but a committee for managing the common affairs of the whole bourgeoisie.

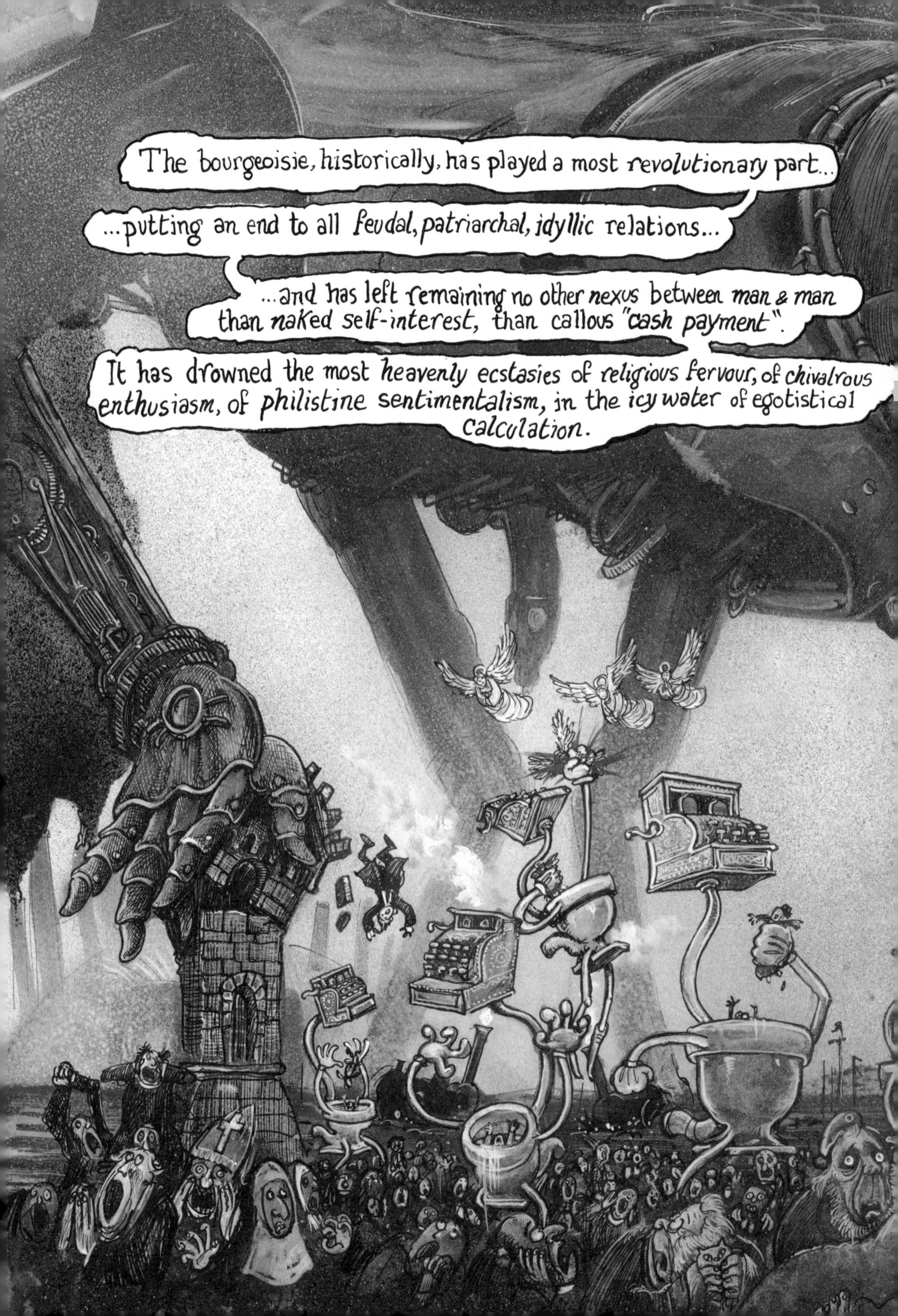
The bourgeoisie, historically, has played a most revolutionary part...
...putting an end to all feudal, patriarchal, idyllic relations...
...and has left remaining no other nexus between man & man than naked self-interest, than callous "cash payment".
It has drowned the most heavenly ecstasies of religious fervour, of chivalrous enthusiasm, of philistine sentimentalism, in the icy water of egotistical calculation.

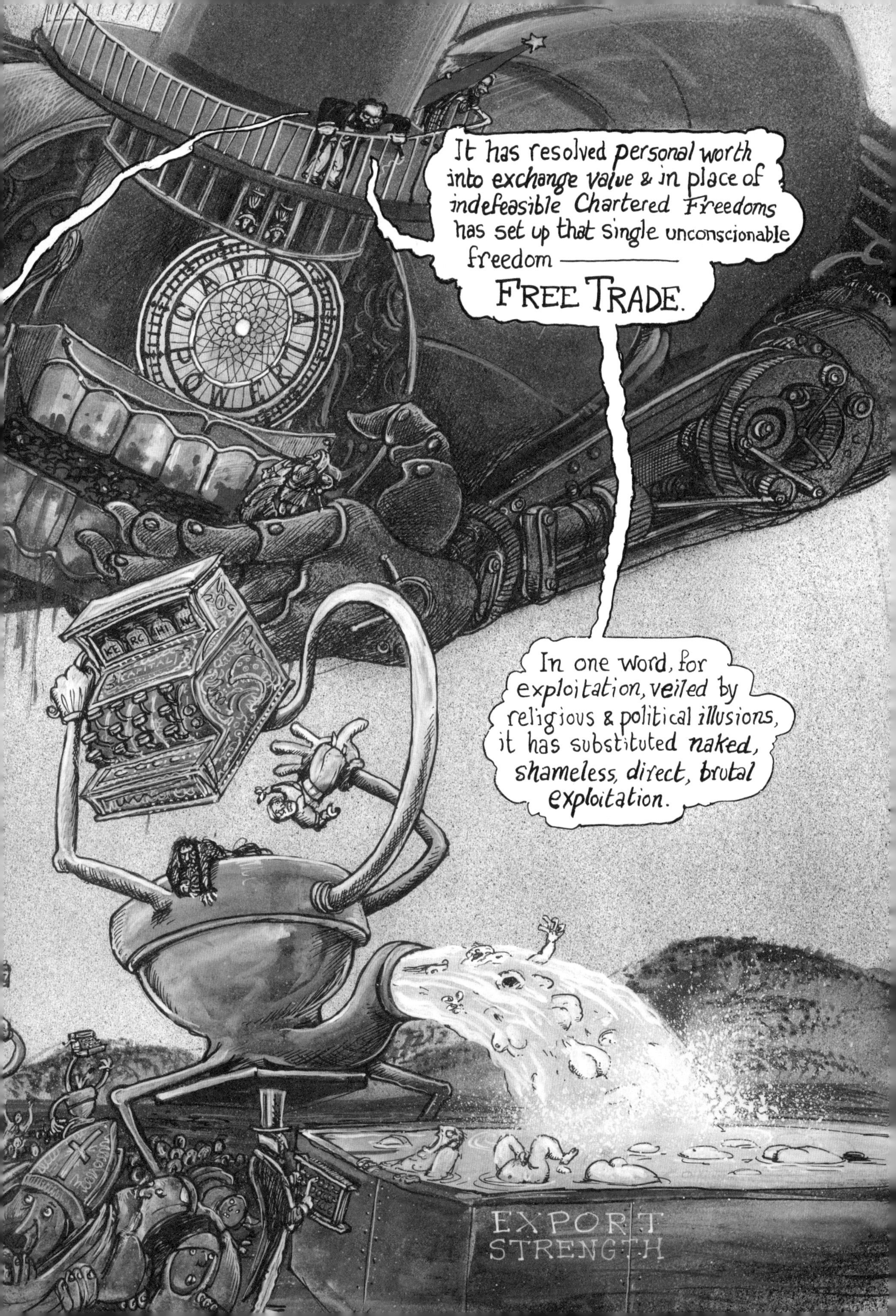
It has resolved personal worth into exchange value & in place of indefeasible Chartered Freedoms has set up that single unconscionable freedom —— FREE TRADE.
In one word, for exploitation, veiled by religious & political illusions, it has substituted naked, shameless, direct, brutal exploitation.
EXPORT STRENGTH

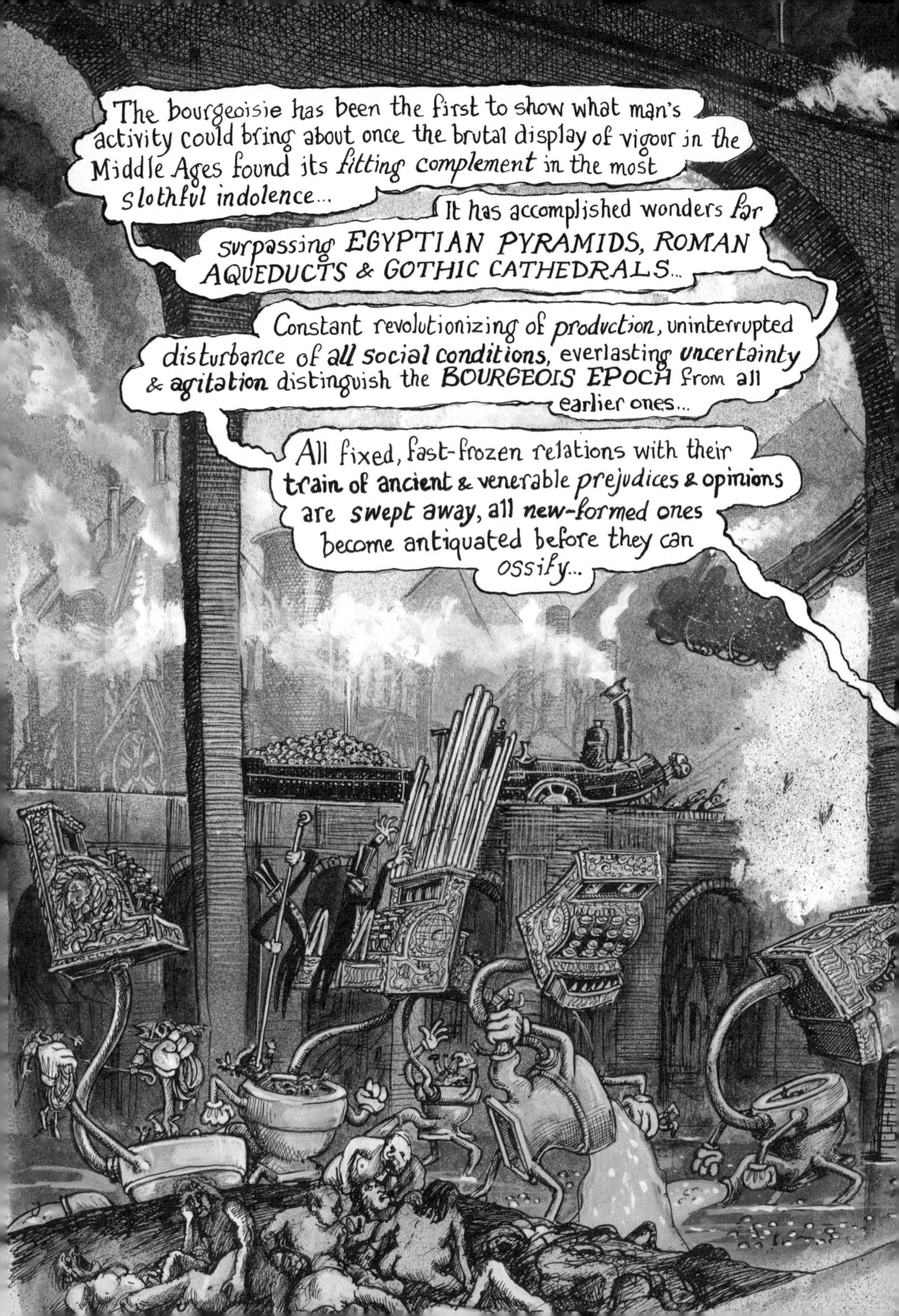
The bourgeoisie has been the first to show what man's activity could bring about once the brutal display of vigour in the Middle Ages found its *fitting complement* in the most *slothful indolence*...
It has accomplished wonders *far surpassing* EGYPTIAN PYRAMIDS, ROMAN AQUEDUCTS & GOTHIC CATHEDRALS...
Constant revolutionizing of *production*, uninterrupted disturbance of **all social conditions**, everlasting *uncertainty* & **agitation** distinguish the BOURGEOIS EPOCH from all earlier ones...
All fixed, fast-frozen relations with their **train of ancient** & venerable *prejudices* & **opinions** are *swept away*, all *new-formed* ones become antiquated before they can *ossify*...

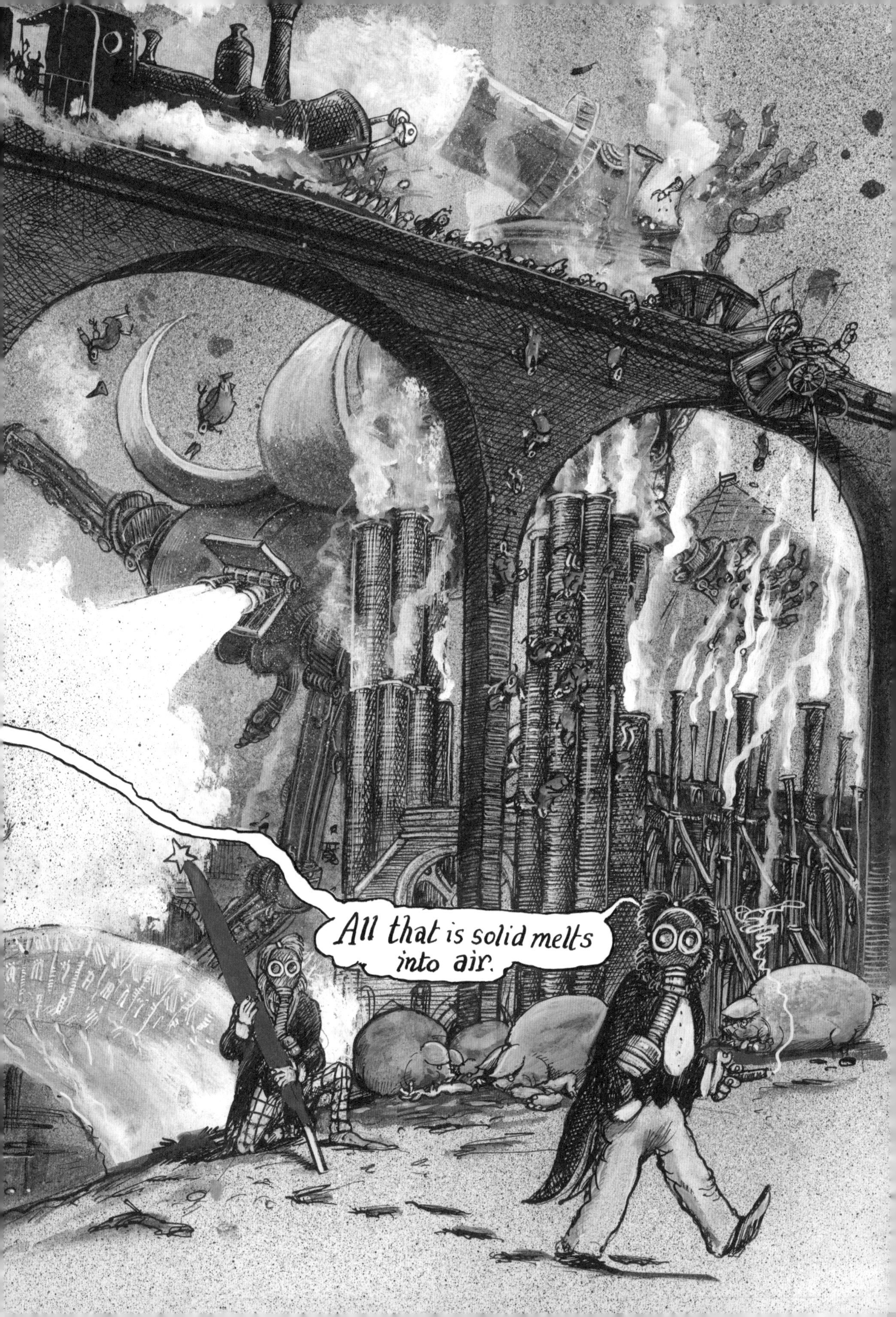
All that is solid melts into air.

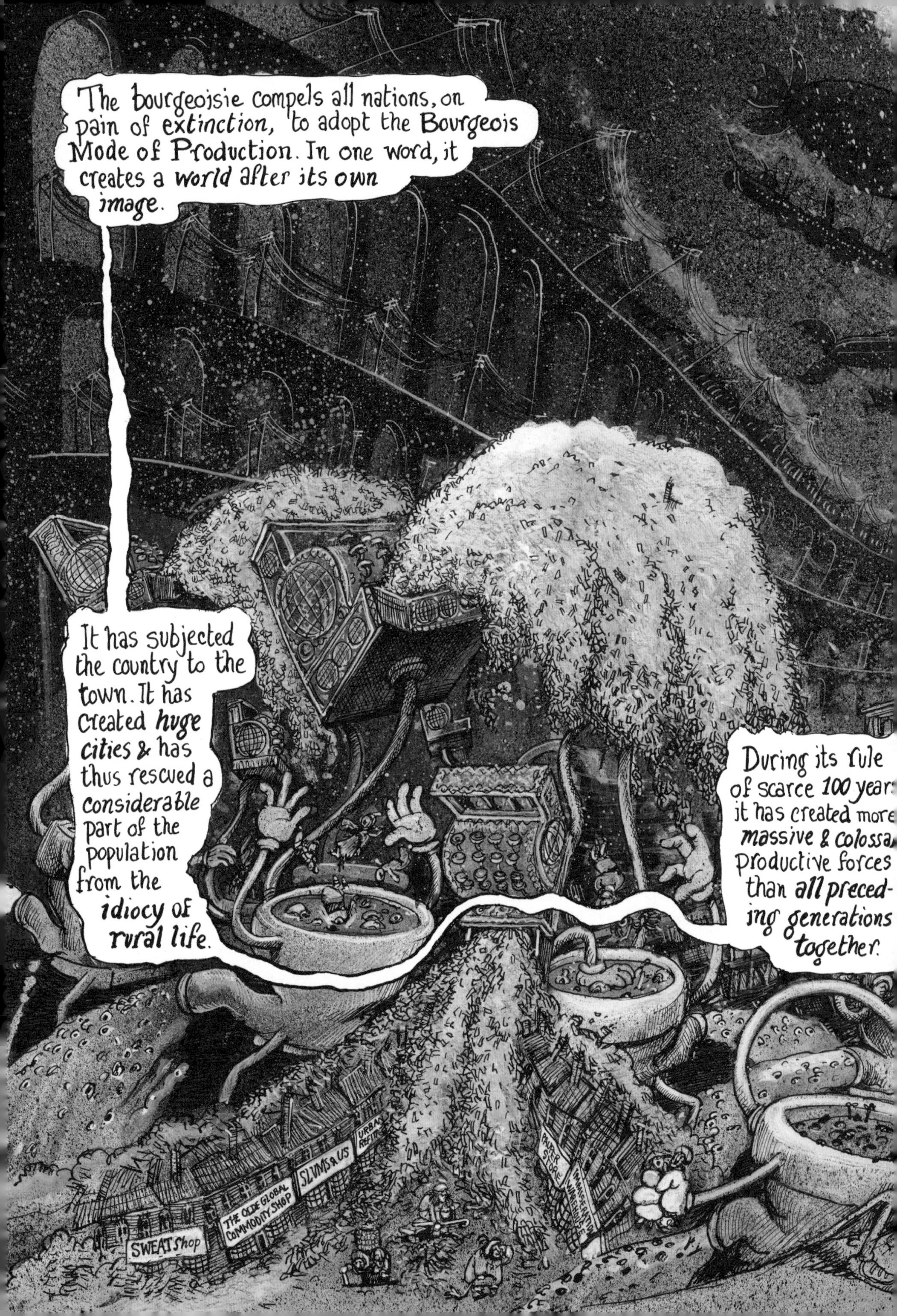

The bourgeoisie compels all nations, on pain of *extinction,* to adopt the Bourgeois Mode of Production. In one word, it creates a *world* after its *own image.*
It has subjected the country to the town. It has created ***huge cities*** & has thus rescued a *considerable* part of the population from the ***idiocy*** of ***rural life.***
During its rule of scarce **100** year it has created more *massive* & Colossa productive forces than ***all*** ***preceding generations together.***
SWEAT Shop
THE OLDE GLOBAL COMMODITY SHOP
SLUMS R US
URBAN
PAUPER STORE
IMMIGRATION WAREHOUSE

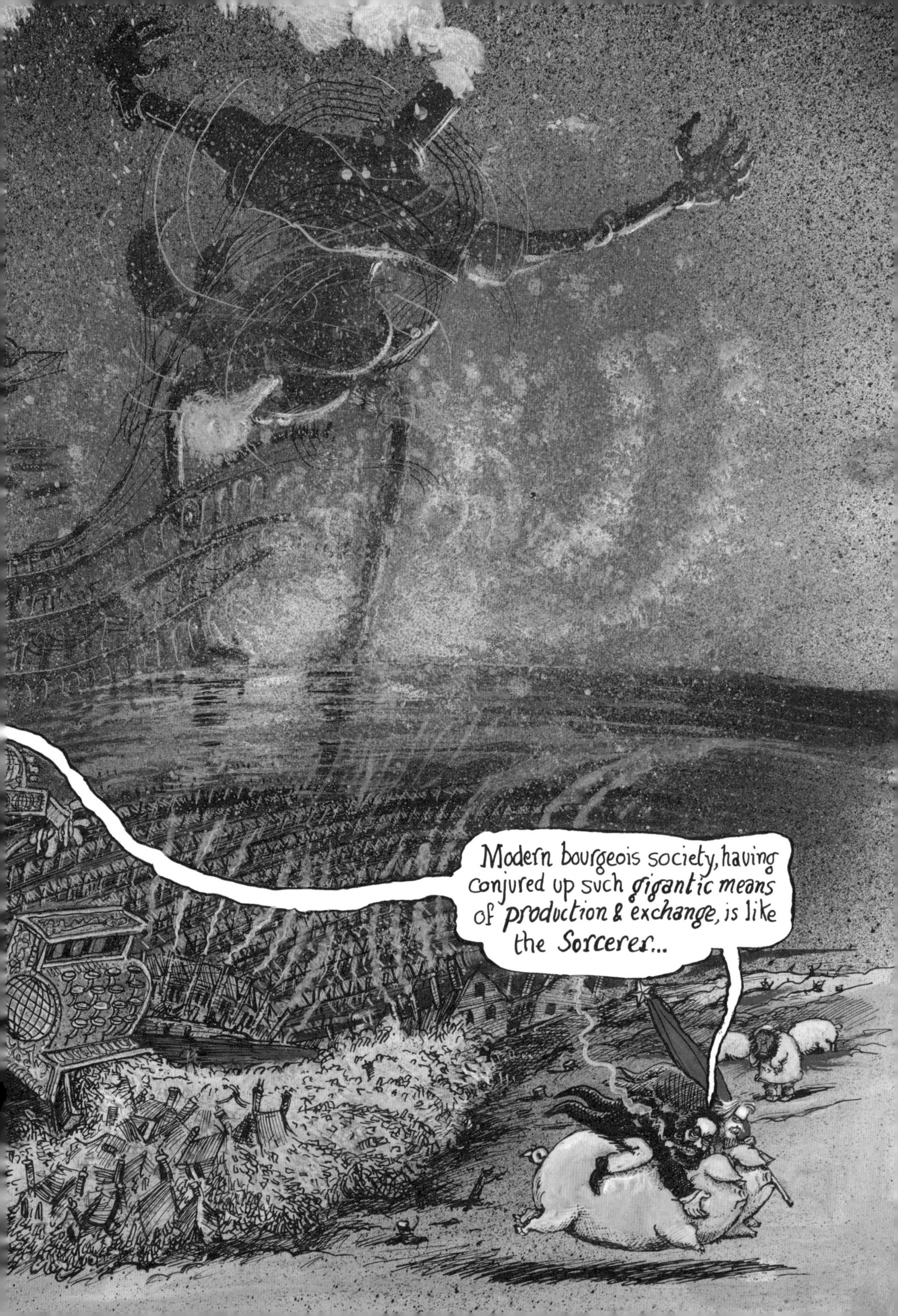
Modern bourgeois society, having conjured up such gigantic means of production & exchange, is like the Sorcerer...

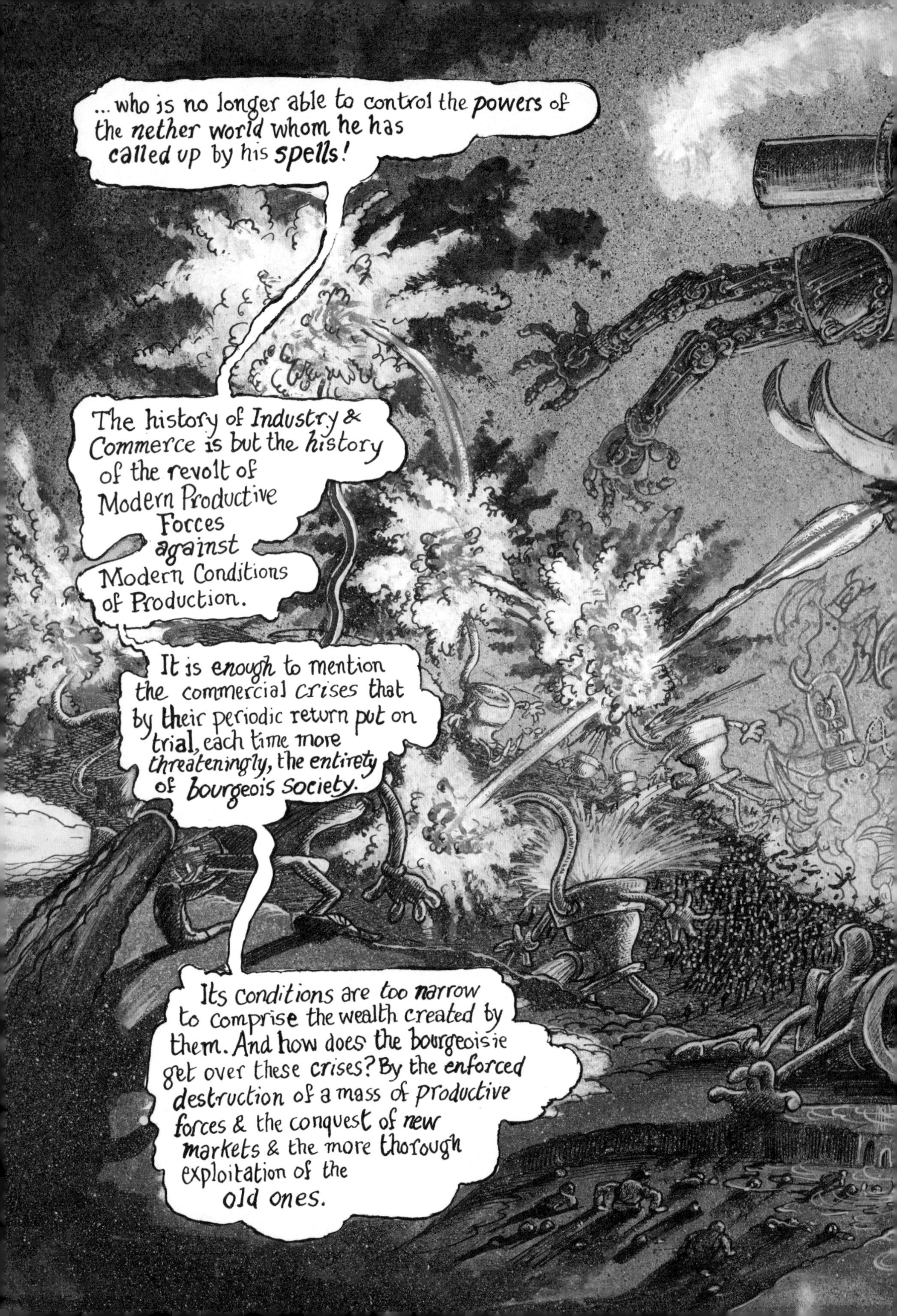
...who is no longer able to control the powers of the nether world whom he has called up by his spells!
The history of Industry & Commerce is but the history of the revolt of Modern Productive Forces against Modern Conditions of Production.
It is enough to mention the commercial crises that by their periodic return put on trial, each time more threateningly, the entirety of bourgeois society.
Its conditions are too narrow to comprise the wealth created by them. And how does the bourgeoisie get over these crises? By the enforced destruction of a mass of productive forces & the conquest of new markets & the more thorough exploitation of the old ones.

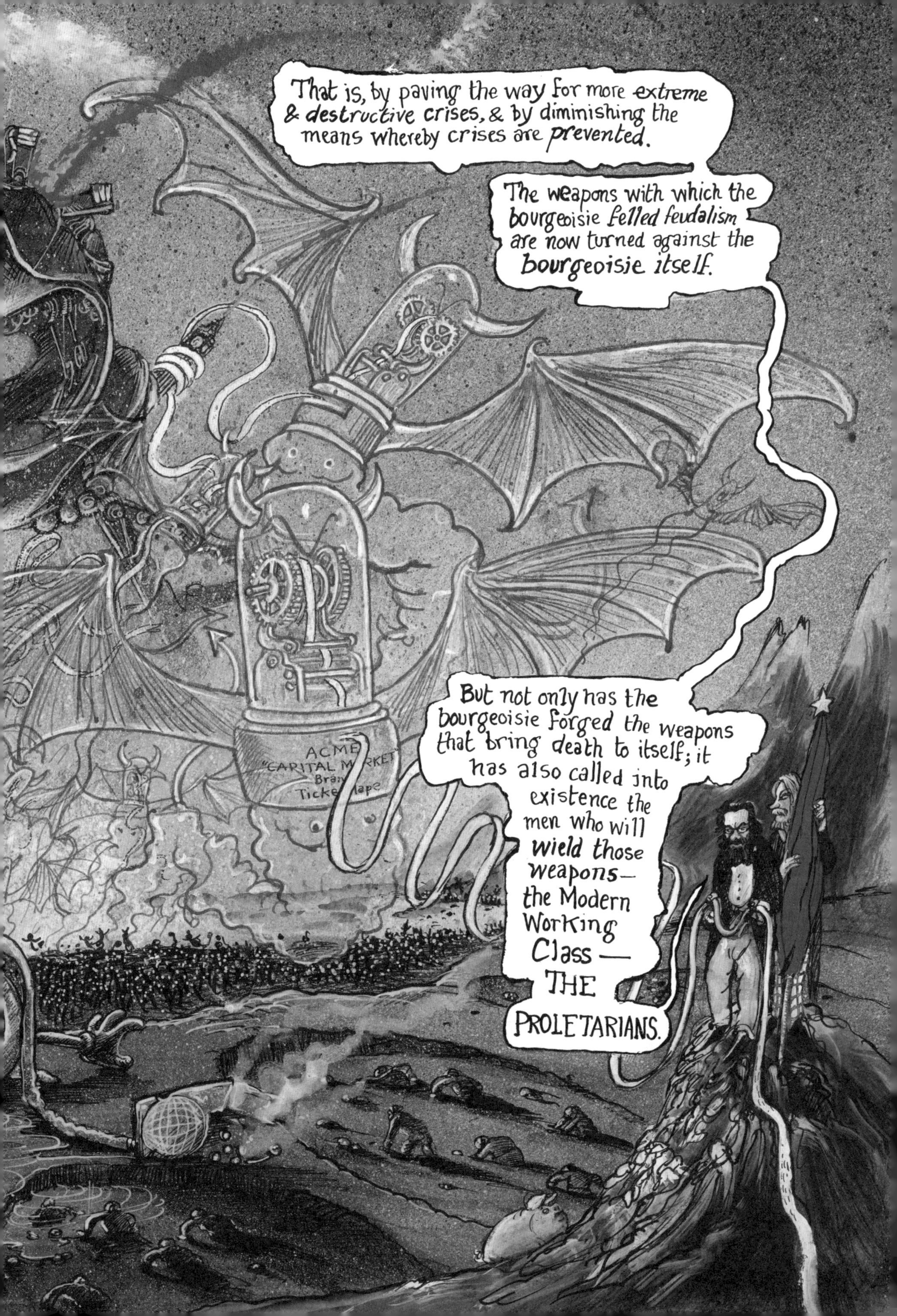
That is, by paving the way for more *extreme* & *destructive* crises, & by diminishing the means whereby crises are *prevented*.
The weapons with which the bourgeoisie *felled feudalism* are now turned against the **bourgeoisie itself**.
ACME
But not only has the bourgeoisie forged the weapons that bring death to itself; it has also called into existence the men who will **wield those weapons** — the Modern Working Class — THE PROLETARIANS.

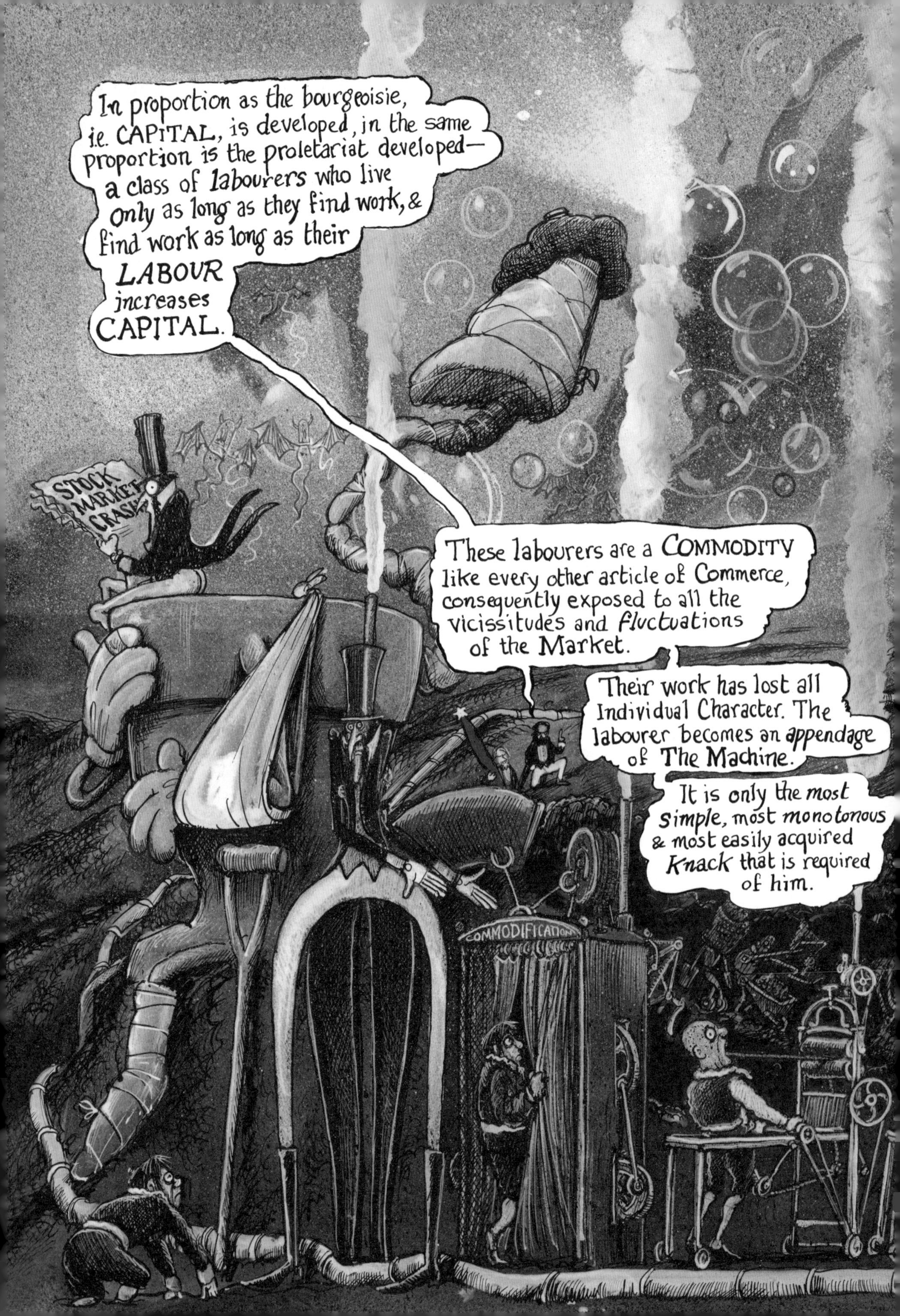

In proportion as the bourgeoisie, i.e. CAPITAL, is developed, in the same proportion is the proletariat developed— a class of labourers who live only as long as they find work, & find work as long as their LABOUR increases CAPITAL.
STOCK MARKET CRASH
These labourers are a COMMODITY like every other article of Commerce, consequently exposed to all the vicissitudes and fluctuations of the Market.
Their work has lost all Individual Character. The labourer becomes an appendage of The Machine.
It is only the most simple, most monotonous & most easily acquired Knack that is required of him.
COMMODIFICATION

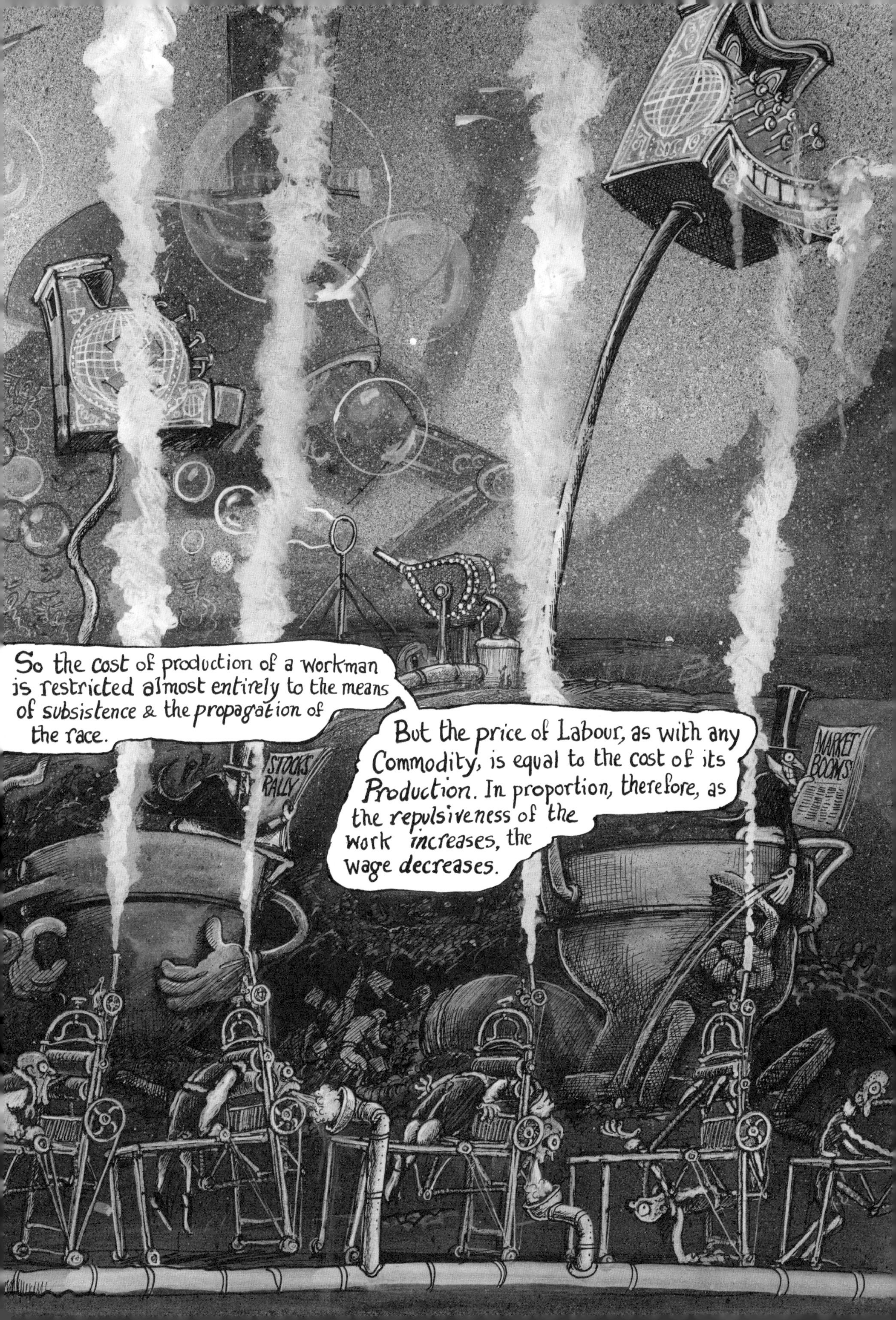

So the cost of production of a workman is restricted almost entirely to the means of subsistence & the propagation of the race.
STOCKS RALLY
But the price of Labour, as with any Commodity, is equal to the cost of its Production. In proportion, therefore, as the repulsiveness of the work increases, the wage decreases.
MARKET BOOMS

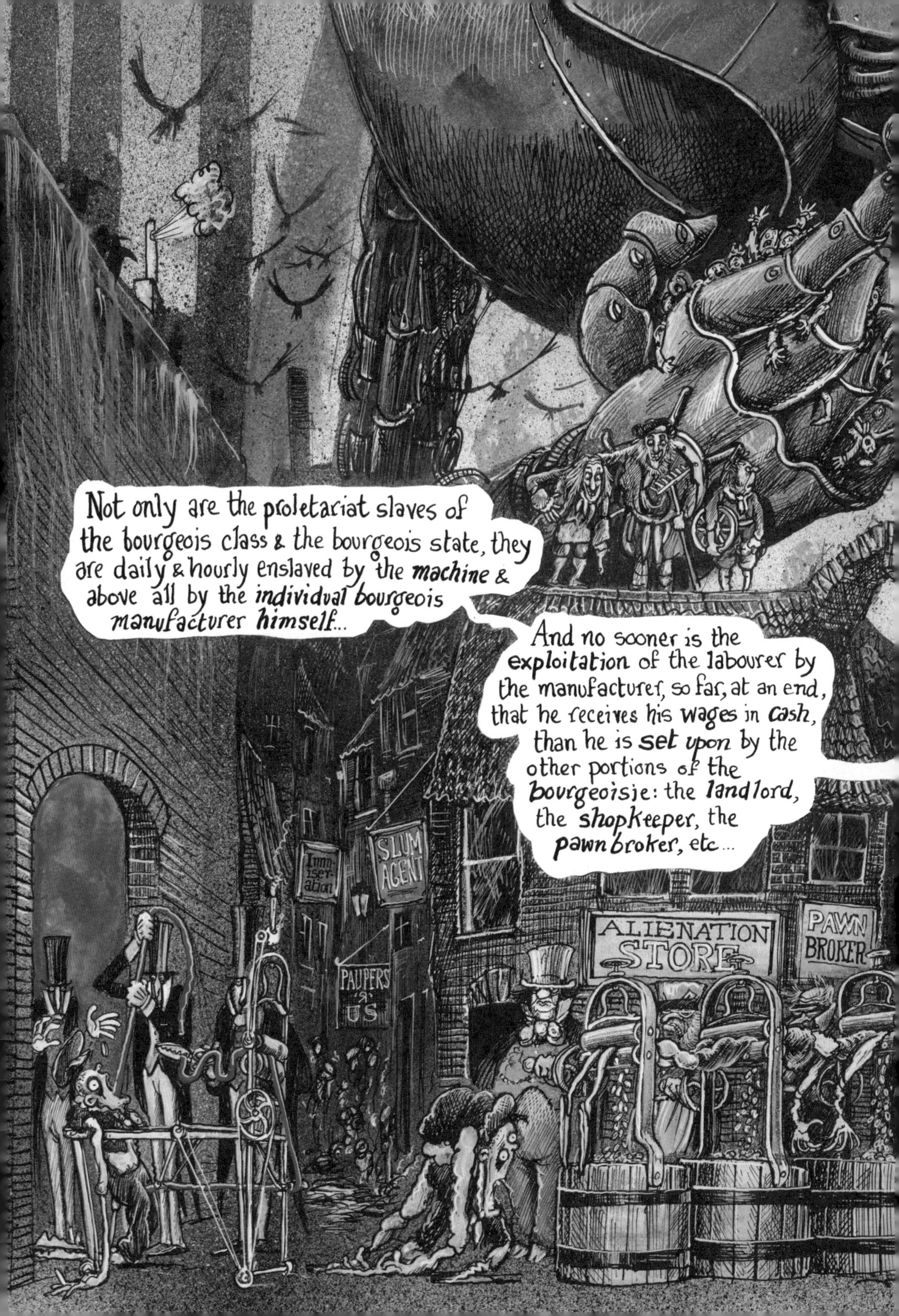

Not only are the proletariat slaves of the bourgeois class & the bourgeois state, they are daily & hourly enslaved by the ***machine*** & above all by the ***individual bourgeois manufacturer himself***...
And no sooner is the **exploitation** of the labourer by the manufacturer, so far, at an end, that he receives his **wages** in **cash**, than he is **set upon** by the other portions of the ***bourgeoisie***: the ***landlord***, the ***shopkeeper***, the ***pawnbroker***, etc...
Immiseration
SLUM AGENT
PAUPERS 'R' US
ALIENATION STORE
PAWN BROKER

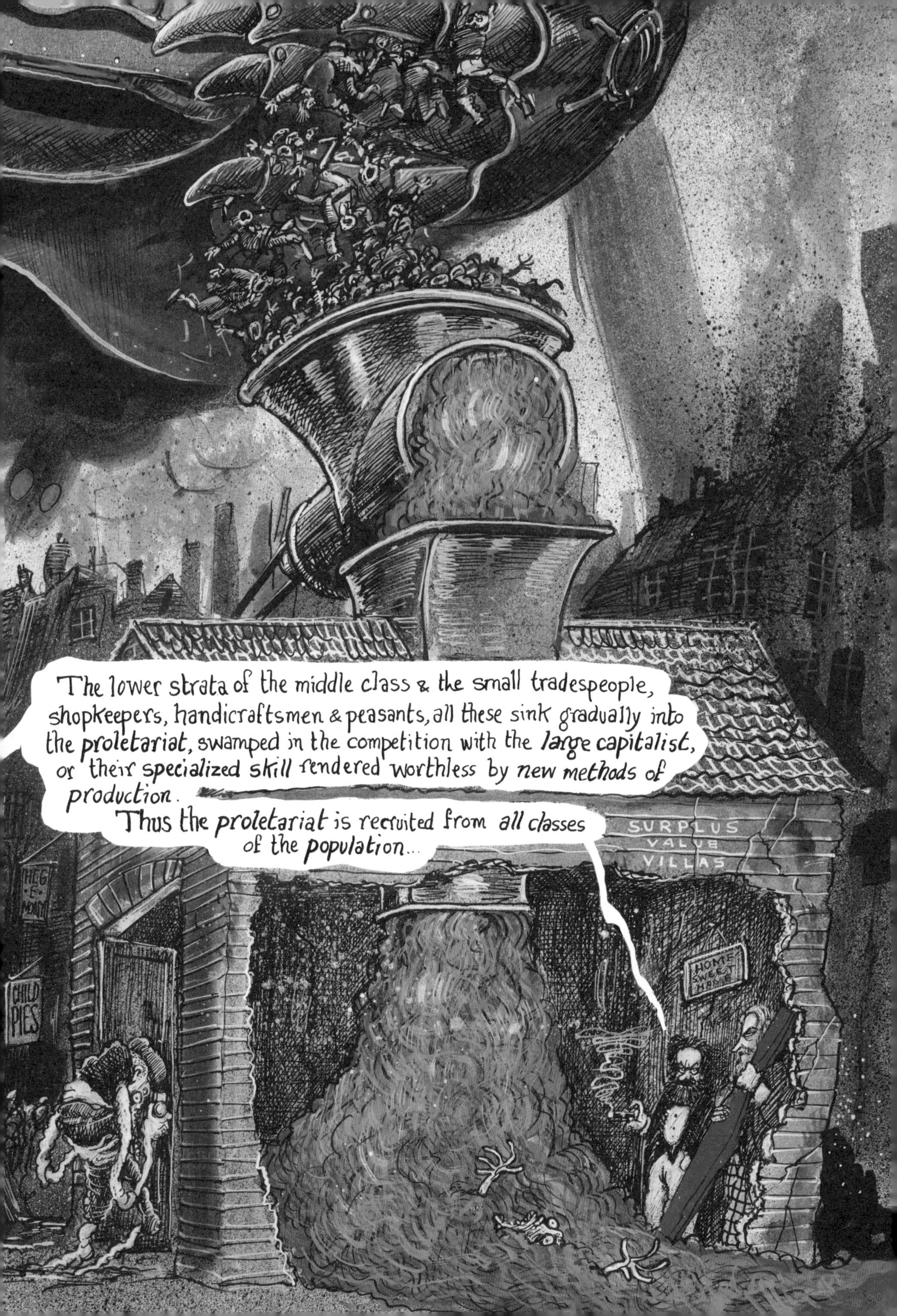

The lower strata of the middle class & the small tradespeople, shopkeepers, handicraftsmen & peasants, all these sink gradually into the *proletariat*, swamped in the competition with the *large capitalist*, or their *specialized skill* rendered worthless by *new methods of production*.
Thus the *proletariat* is recruited from *all classes of the population*...
SURPLUS VALUE VILLAS
HOME SWEET HOME
CHILD PIES

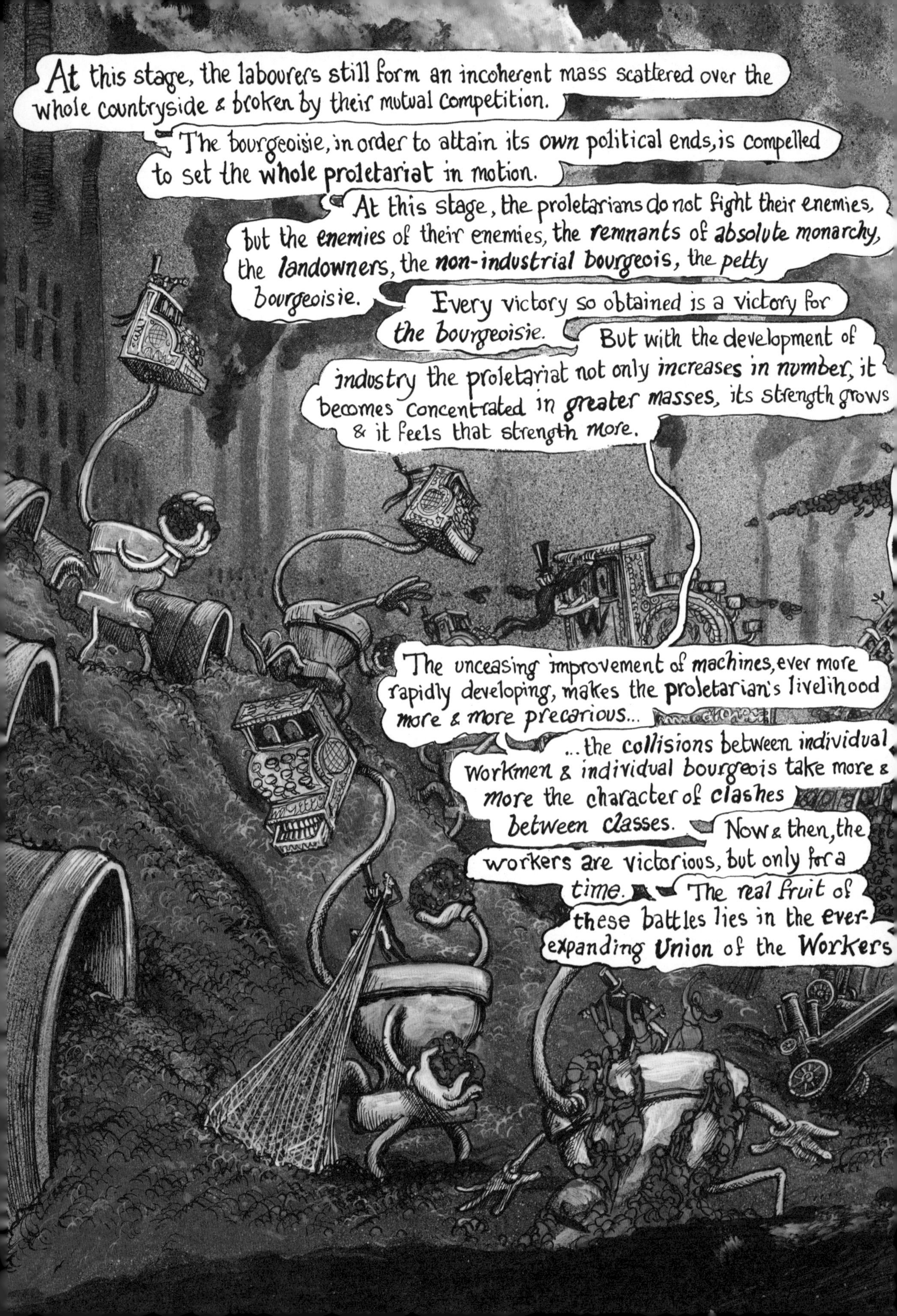
At this stage, the labourers still form an incoherent mass scattered over the whole countryside & broken by their mutual competition.
The bourgeoisie, in order to attain its own political ends, is compelled to set the whole proletariat in motion.
At this stage, the proletarians do not fight their enemies, but the enemies of their enemies, the remnants of absolute monarchy, the landowners, the non-industrial bourgeois, the petty bourgeoisie.
Every victory so obtained is a victory for the bourgeoisie.
But with the development of industry the proletariat not only increases in number, it becomes concentrated in greater masses, its strength grows & it feels that strength more.
The unceasing improvement of machines, ever more rapidly developing, makes the proletarian's livelihood more & more precarious...
...the collisions between individual workmen & individual bourgeois take more & more the character of clashes between classes.
Now & then, the workers are victorious, but only for a time.
The real fruit of these battles lies in the ever-expanding Union of the Workers

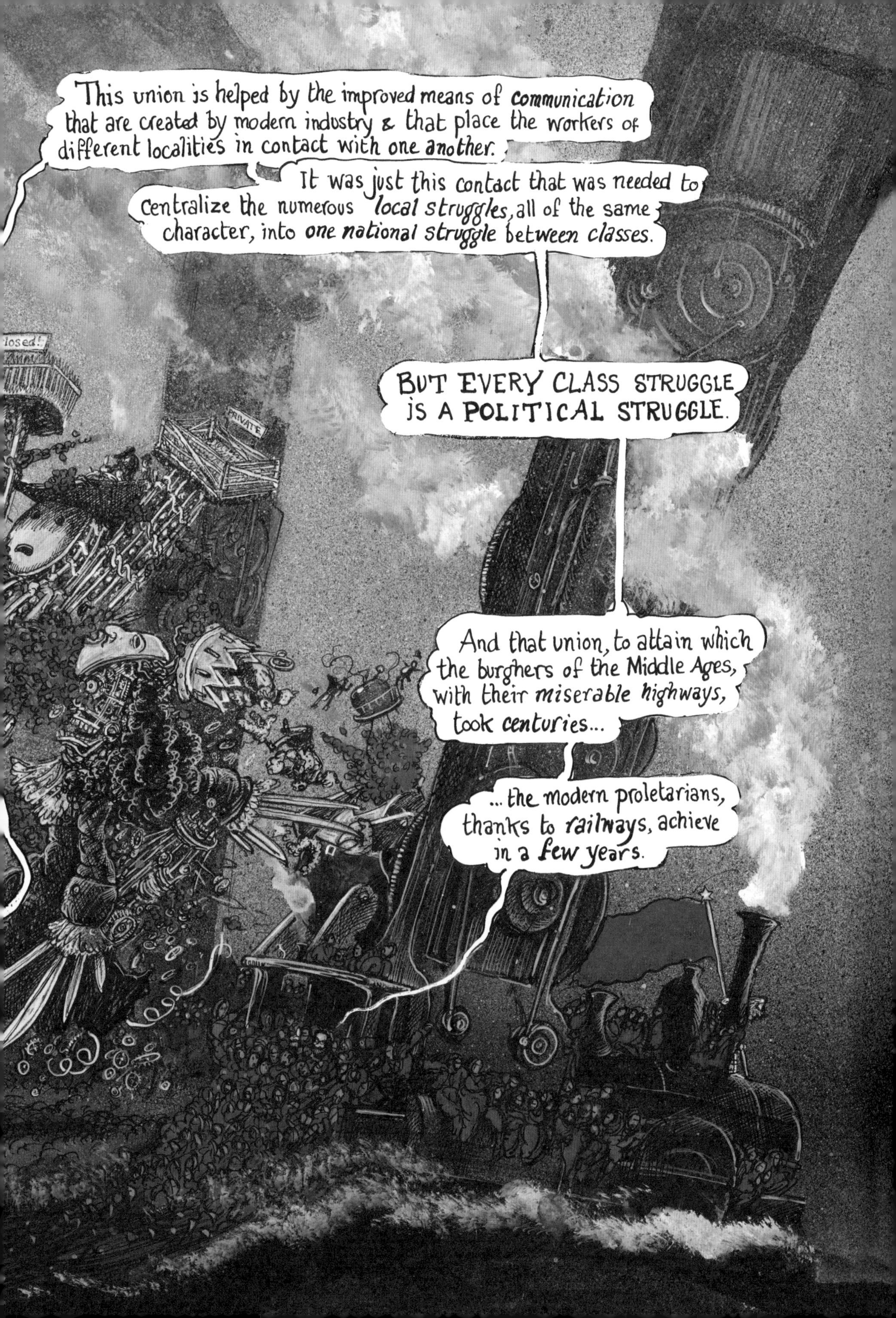
This union is helped by the improved means of communication that are created by modern industry & that place the workers of different localities in contact with one another.
It was just this contact that was needed to centralize the numerous local struggles, all of the same character, into one national struggle between classes.
BUT EVERY CLASS STRUGGLE IS A POLITICAL STRUGGLE.
And that union, to attain which the burghers of the Middle Ages, with their miserable highways, took centuries...
... the modern proletarians, thanks to railways, achieve in a few years.
PRIVATE

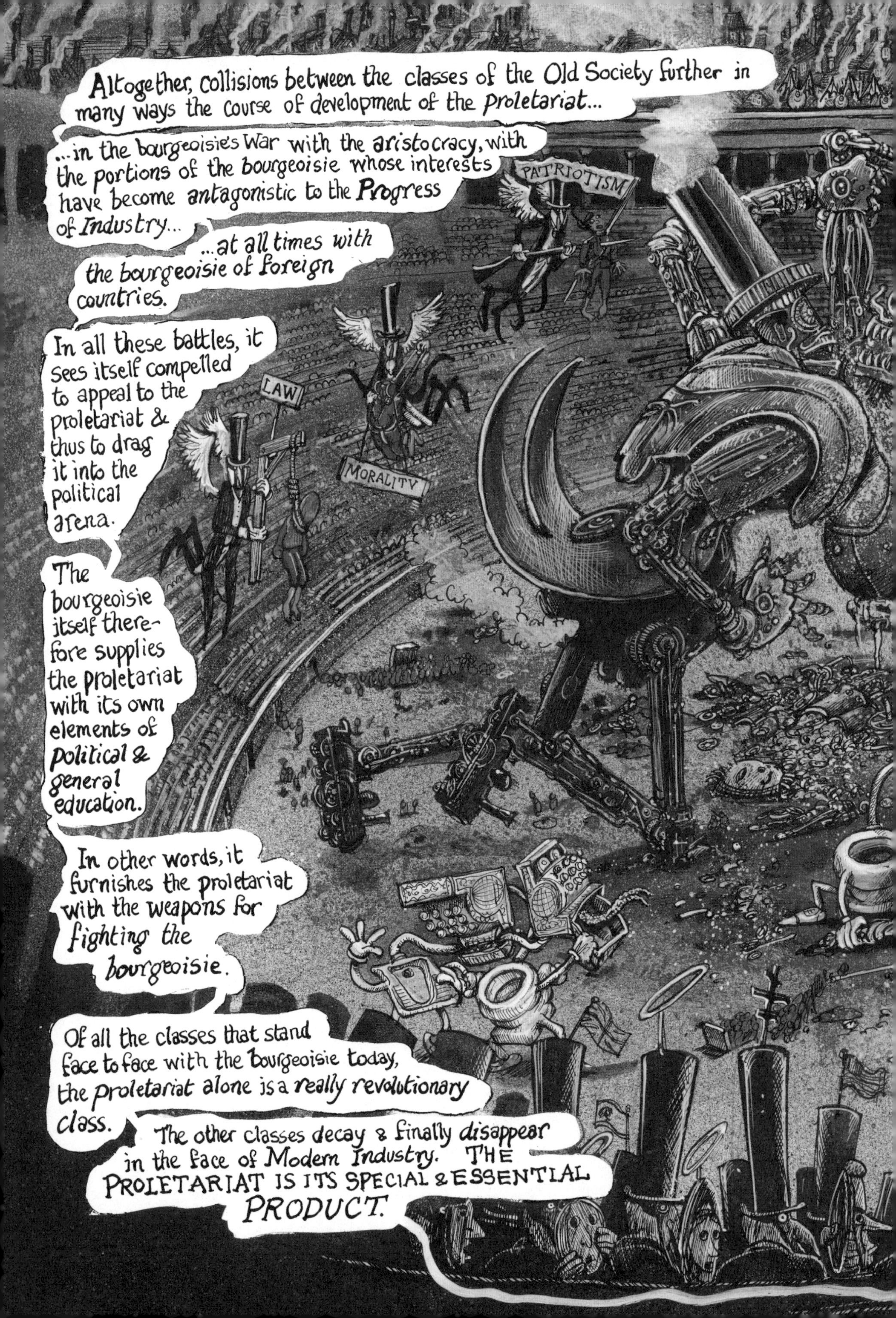
Altogether, collisions between the classes of the Old Society further in many ways the course of development of the *proletariat*...
...in the bourgeoisie's War with the aristocracy, with the portions of the bourgeoisie whose interests have become *antagonistic* to the *Progress* of *Industry*...
...at all times with the bourgeoisie of foreign countries.
PATRIOTISM
LAW
MORALITY
In all these battles, it sees itself compelled to appeal to the proletariat & thus to drag it into the political arena.
The bourgeoisie itself therefore supplies the proletariat with its own elements of *political* & *general education*.
In other words, it furnishes the proletariat with the weapons for *fighting the bourgeoisie*.
Of all the classes that stand face to face with the bourgeoisie today, the *proletariat* alone is a *really revolutionary* class.
The other classes decay & finally *disappear* in the face of Modern Industry. THE PROLETARIAT IS ITS SPECIAL & ESSENTIAL PRODUCT.

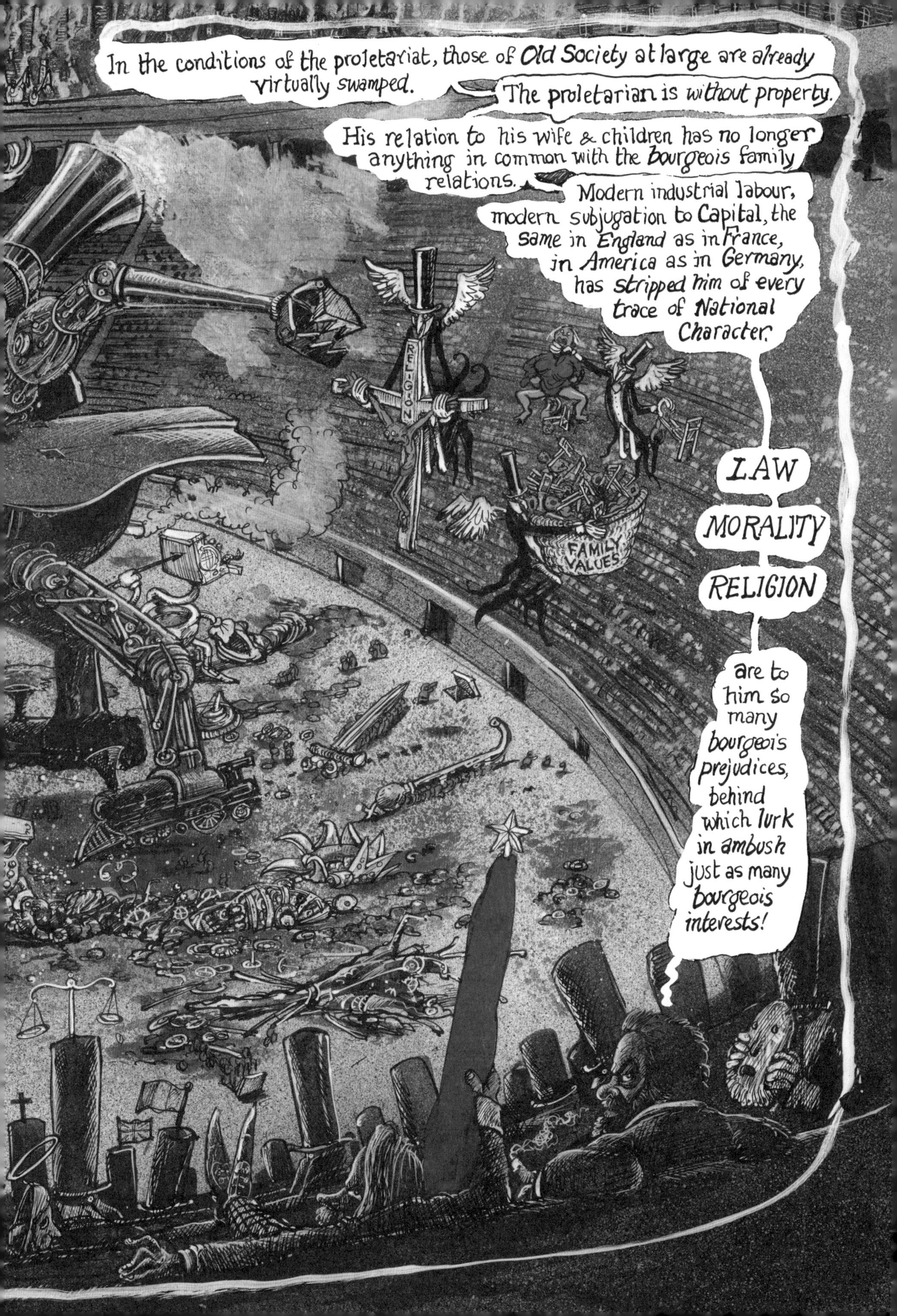
In the conditions of the proletariat, those of Old Society at large are already virtually swamped.
The proletarian is without property.
His relation to his wife & children has no longer anything in common with the bourgeois family relations.
Modern industrial labour, modern subjugation to Capital, the same in England as in France, in America as in Germany, has stripped him of every trace of National Character.
LAW
MORALITY
RELIGION
are to him so many bourgeois prejudices, behind which lurk in ambush just as many bourgeois interests!
RELIGION
FAMILY VALUES

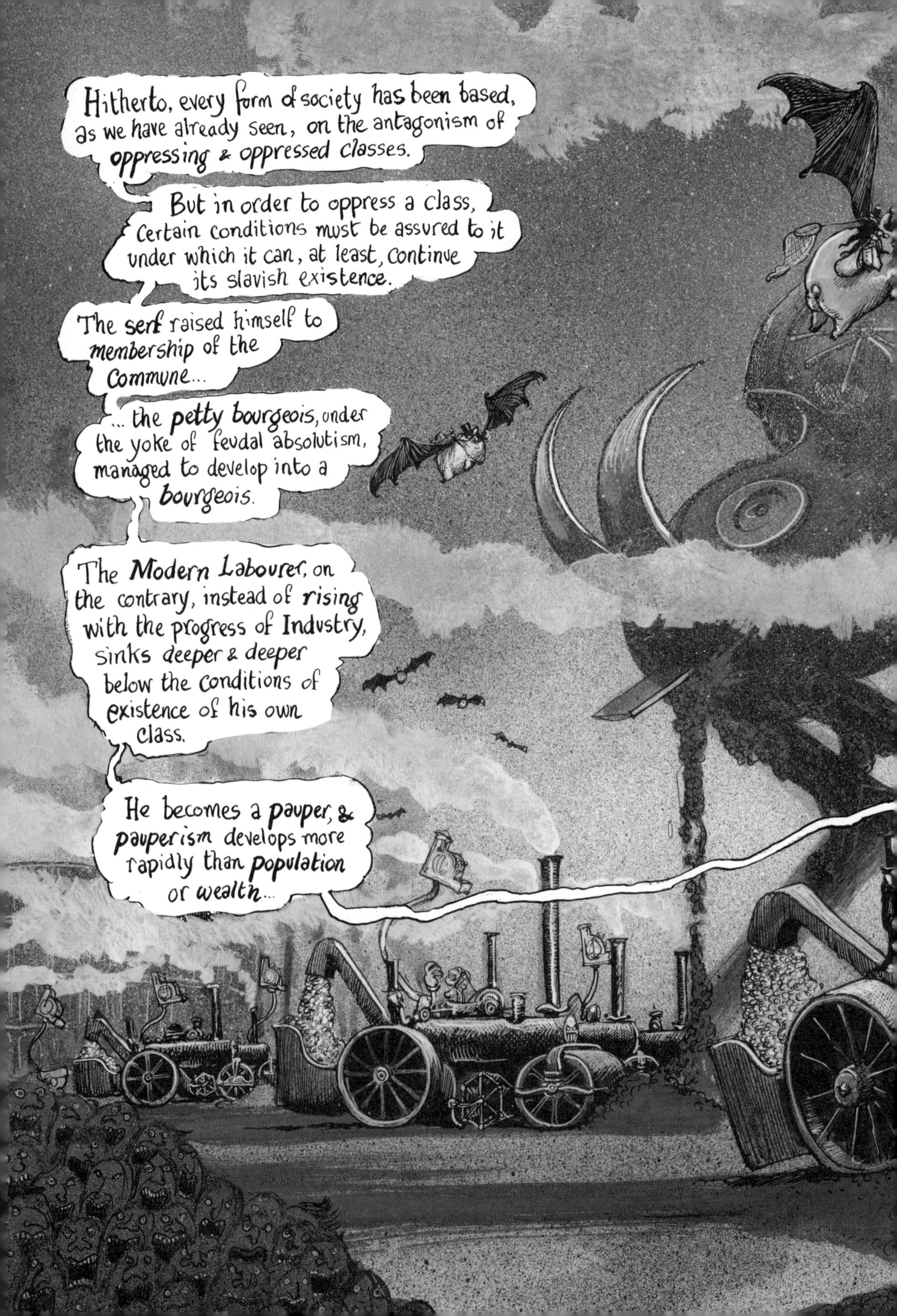
Hitherto, every form of society has been based, as we have already seen, on the antagonism of oppressing & oppressed classes.
But in order to oppress a class, certain conditions must be assured to it under which it can, at least, continue its slavish existence.
The serf raised himself to membership of the Commune...
... the petty bourgeois, under the yoke of feudal absolutism, managed to develop into a bourgeois.
The Modern Labourer, on the contrary, instead of rising with the progress of Industry, sinks deeper & deeper below the conditions of existence of his own class.
He becomes a pauper, & pauperism develops more rapidly than population or wealth...

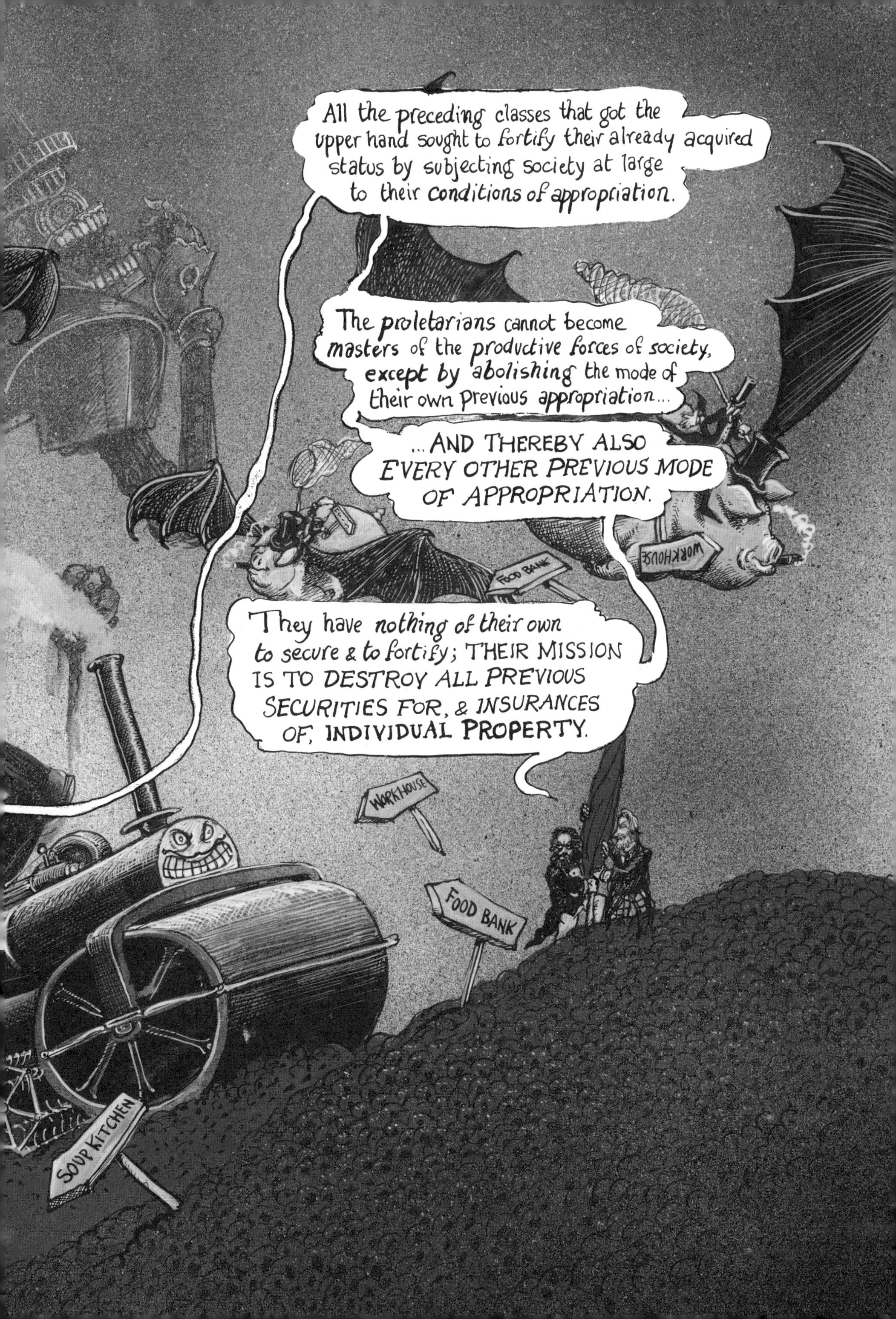
All the preceding classes that got the upper hand sought to fortify their already acquired status by subjecting society at large to their conditions of appropriation.
The proletarians cannot become masters of the productive forces of society, except by abolishing the mode of their own previous appropriation...
...AND THEREBY ALSO EVERY OTHER PREVIOUS MODE OF APPROPRIATION.
They have nothing of their own to secure & to fortify; THEIR MISSION IS TO DESTROY ALL PREVIOUS SECURITIES FOR, & INSURANCES OF, INDIVIDUAL PROPERTY.
FOOD BANK
WORKHOUSE
WORKHOUSE
FOOD BANK
SOUP KITCHEN

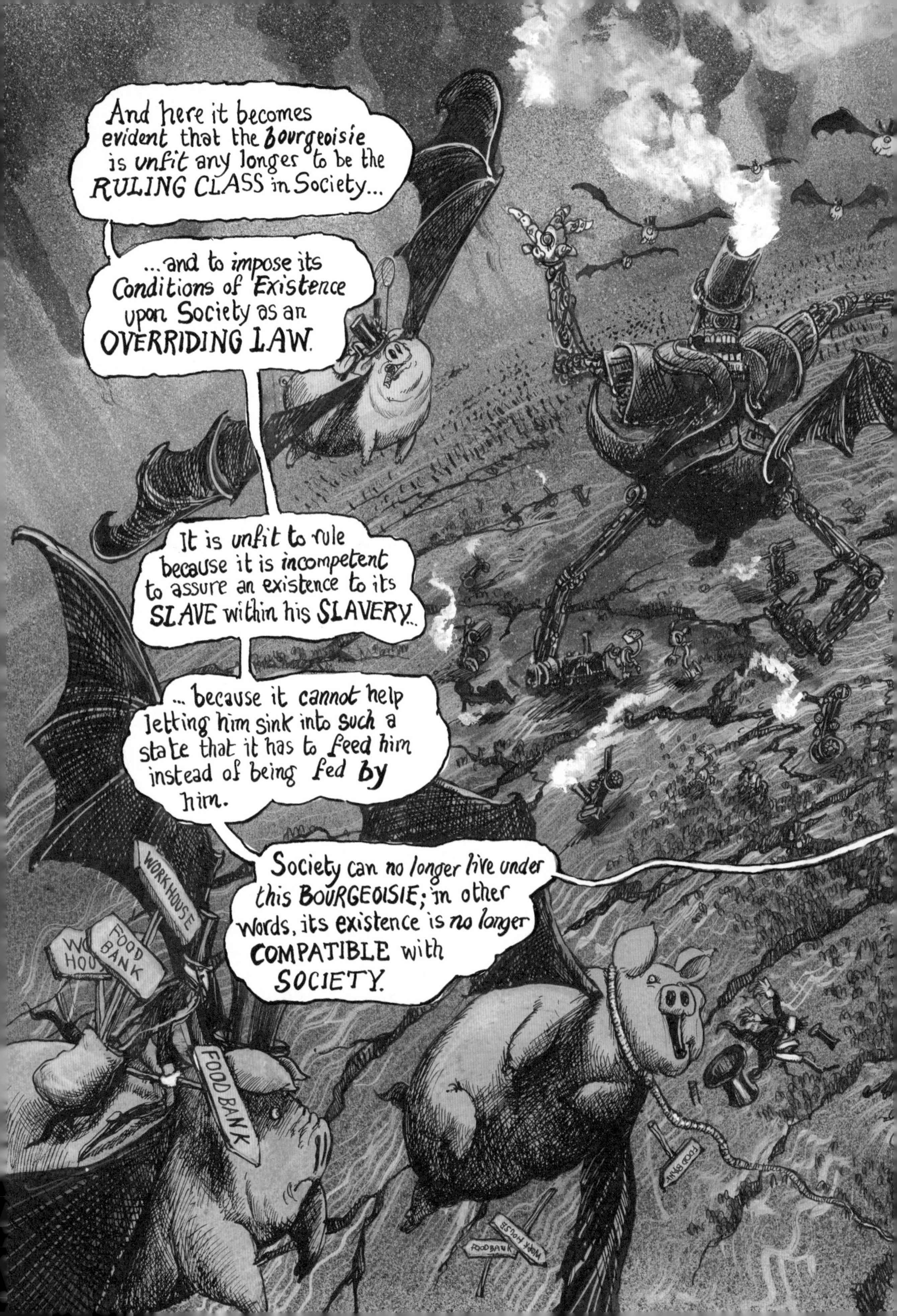
And here it becomes evident that the Bourgeoisie is unfit any longer to be the RULING CLASS in Society...
...and to impose its Conditions of Existence upon Society as an OVERRIDING LAW.
It is unfit to rule because it is incompetent to assure an existence to its SLAVE within his SLAVERY...
... because it cannot help letting him sink into such a state that it has to feed him instead of being fed by him.
Society can no longer live under this BOURGEOISIE; in other words, its existence is no longer COMPATIBLE with SOCIETY.
WORKHOUSE
FOOD BANK
FOOD BANK
FOOD BANK
WORK HOUSE

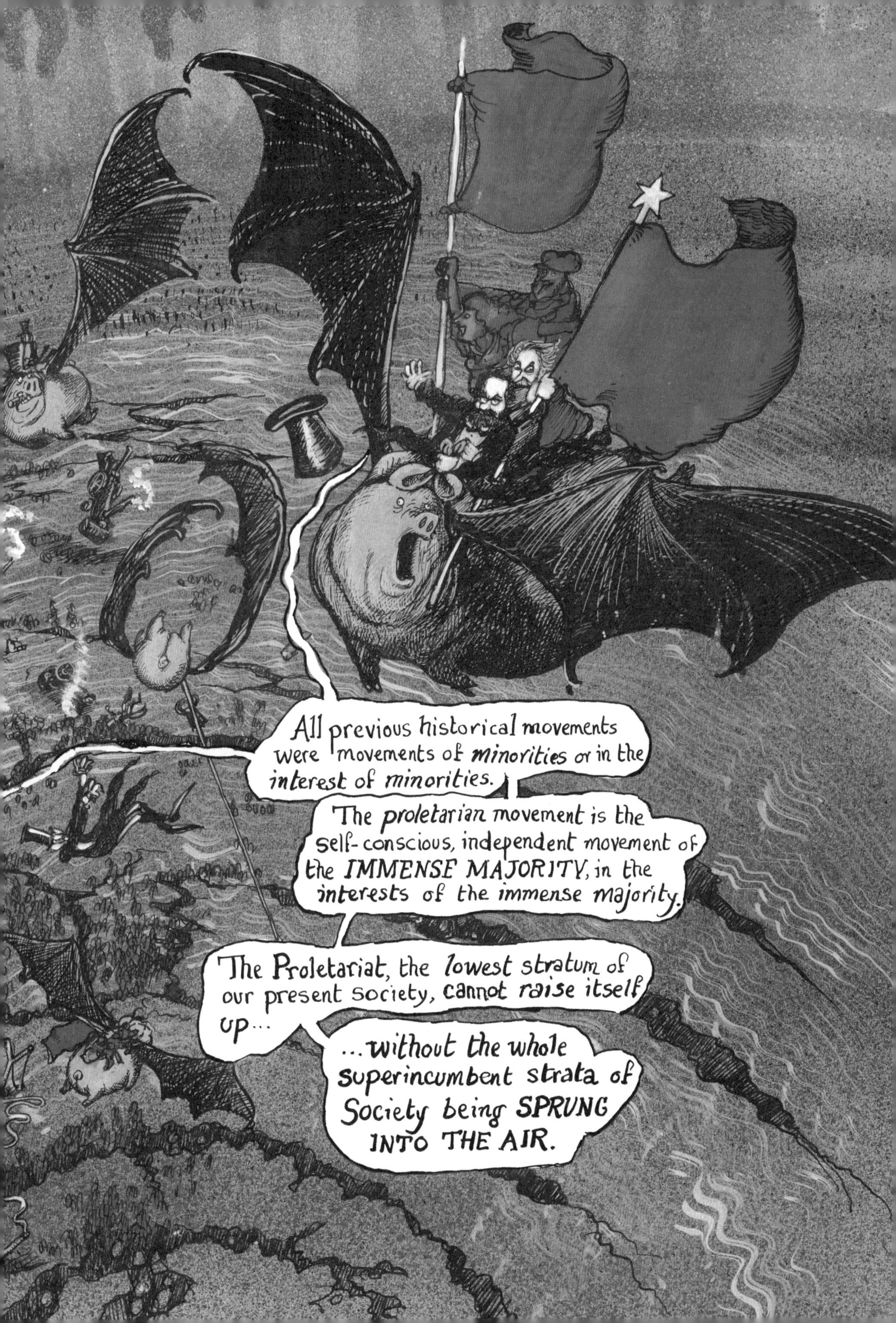
All previous historical movements were movements of minorities or in the interest of minorities.
The proletarian movement is the self-conscious, independent movement of the IMMENSE MAJORITY, in the interests of the immense majority.
The Proletariat, the lowest stratum of our present society, cannot raise itself up...
...without the whole superincumbent strata of Society being SPRUNG INTO THE AIR.

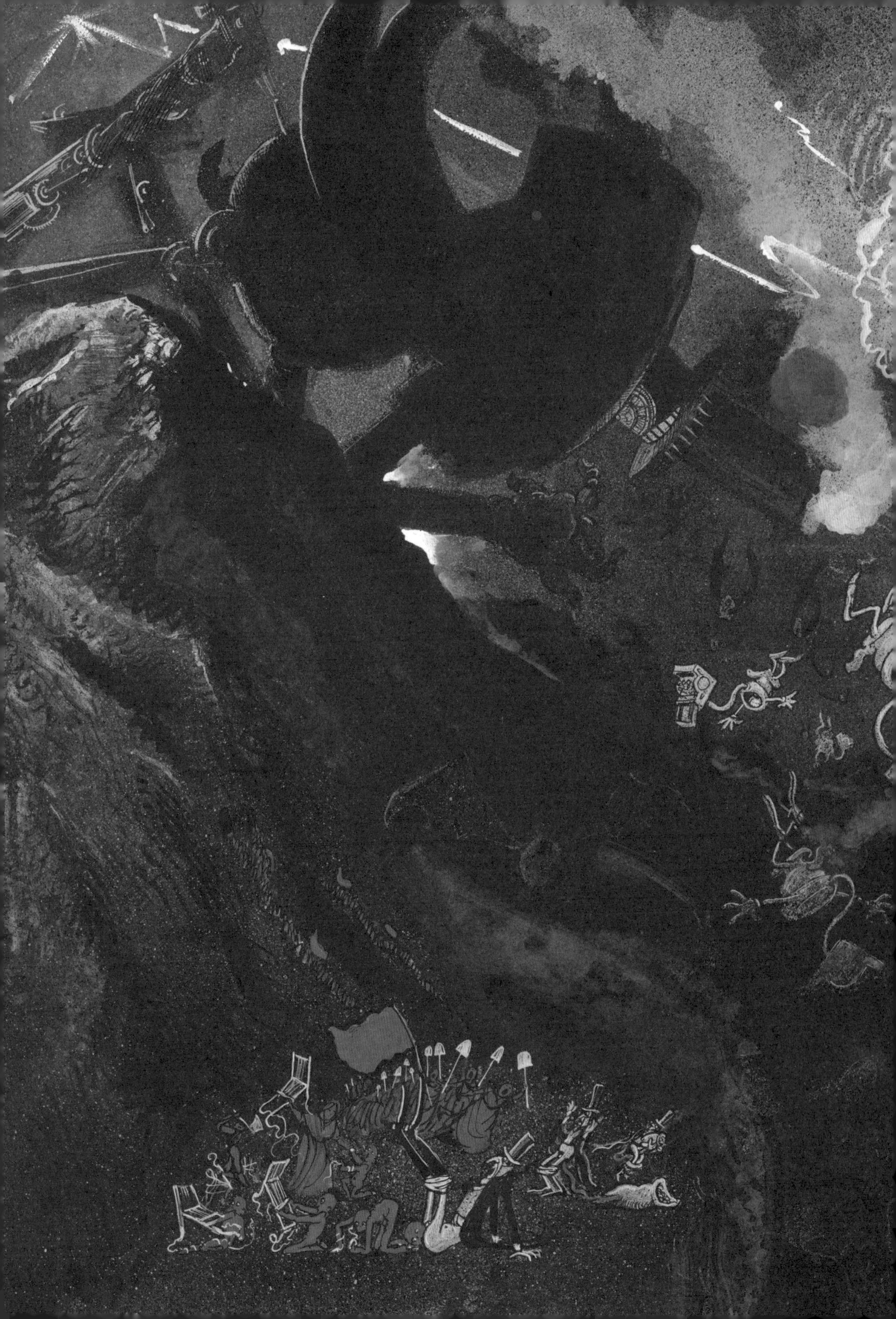

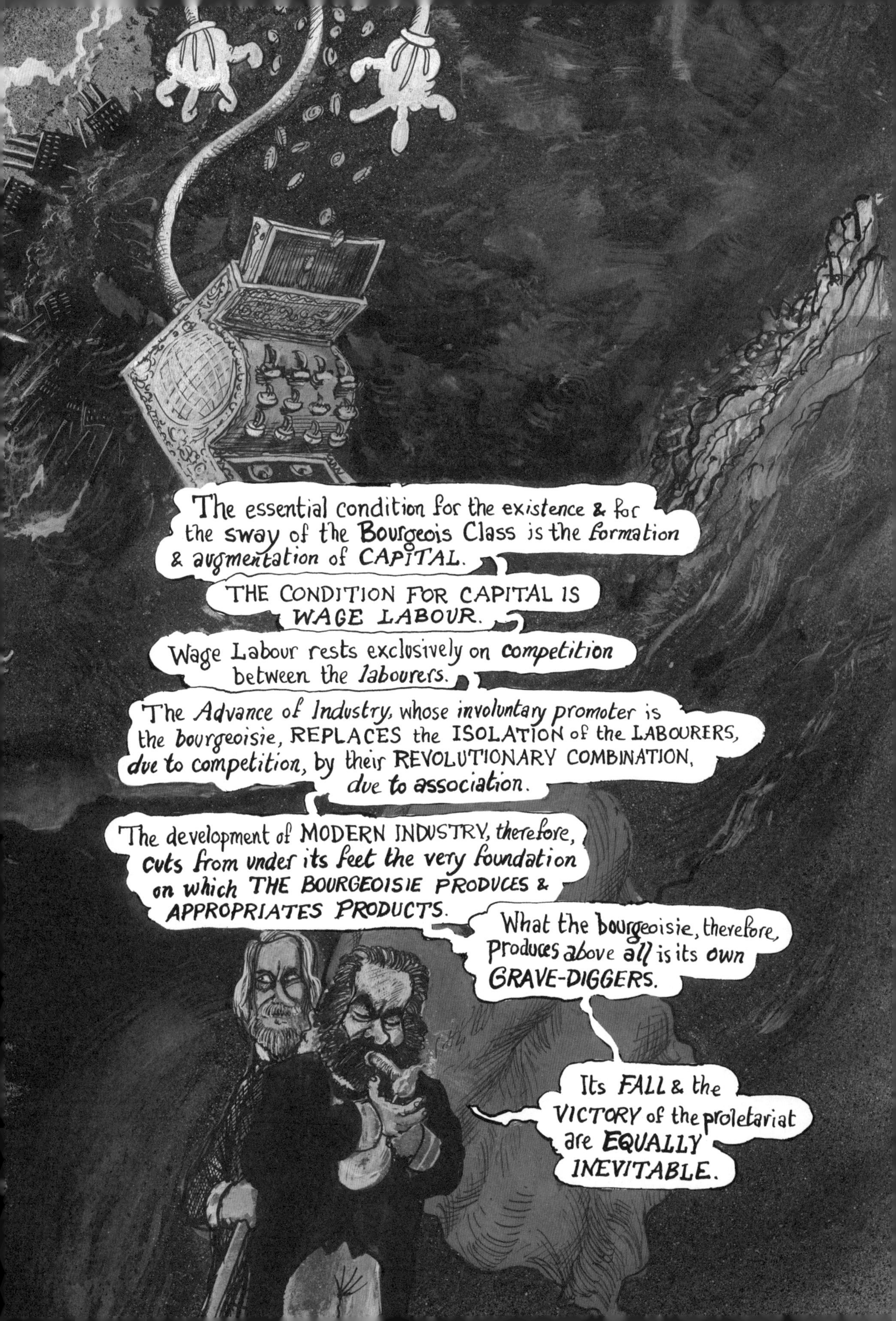
The essential condition for the existence & for the sway of the Bourgeois Class is the formation & augmentation of CAPITAL.
THE CONDITION FOR CAPITAL IS WAGE LABOUR.
Wage Labour rests exclusively on competition between the labourers.
The Advance of Industry, whose involuntary promoter is the bourgeoisie, REPLACES the ISOLATION of the LABOURERS, due to competition, by their REVOLUTIONARY COMBINATION, due to association.
The development of MODERN INDUSTRY, therefore, cuts from under its feet the very foundation on which THE BOURGEOISIE PRODUCES & APPROPRIATES PRODUCTS.
What the bourgeoisie, therefore, produces above all is its own GRAVE-DIGGERS.
Its FALL & the VICTORY of the proletariat are EQUALLY INEVITABLE.

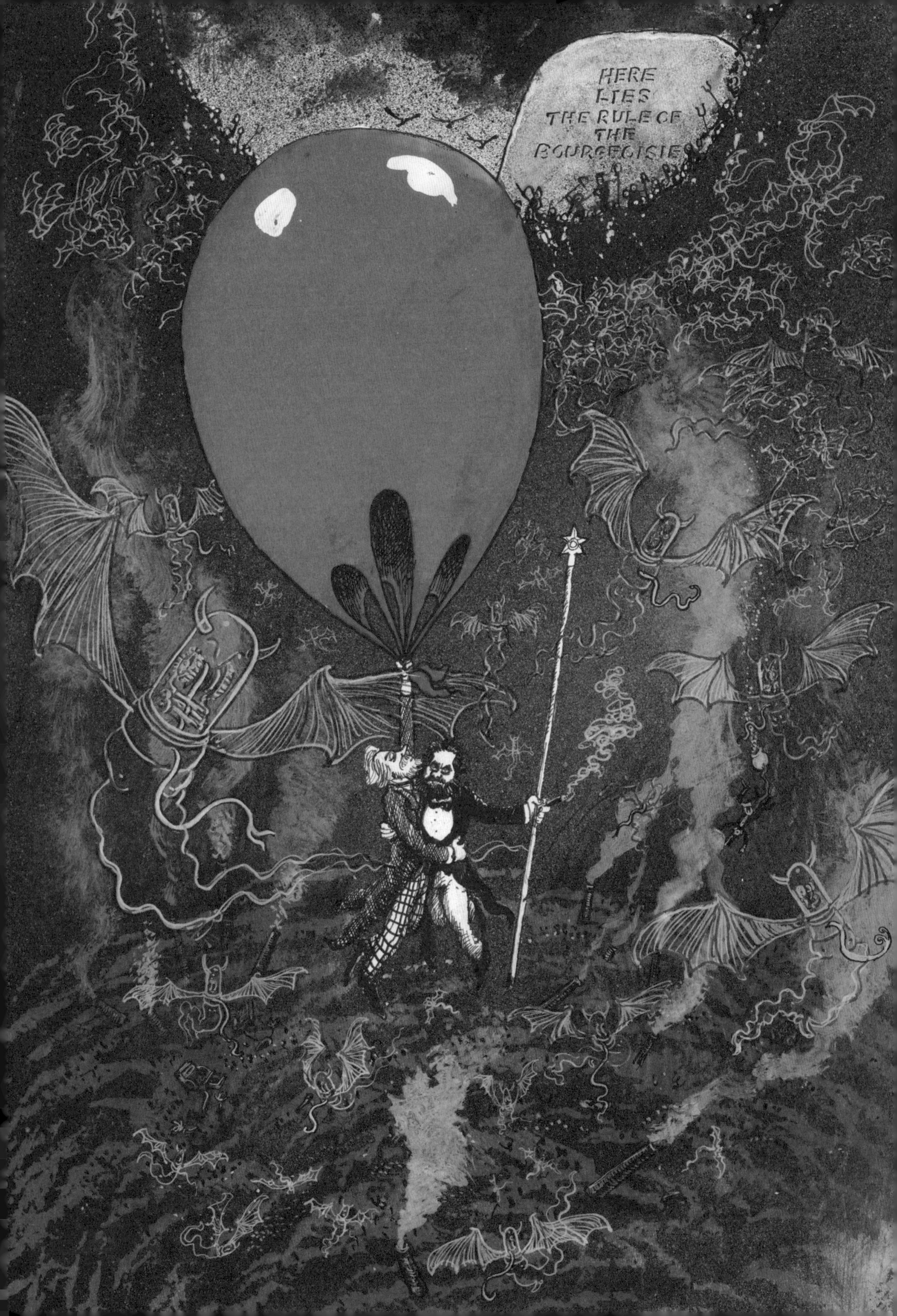
HERE LIES THE RULE OF THE BOURGEOISIE

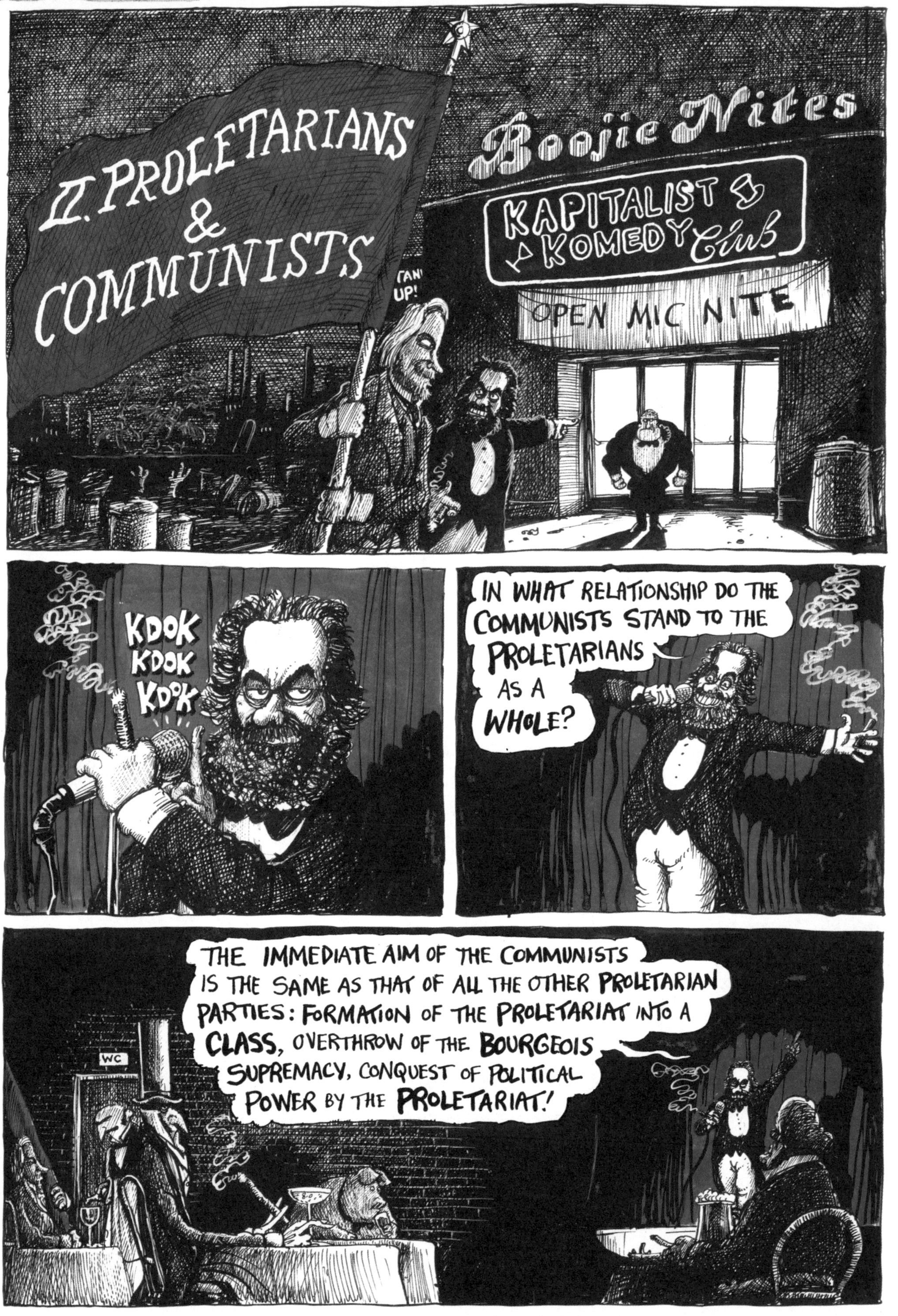
II. PROLETARIANS & COMMUNISTS
Boojie Nites
KAPITALIST KOMEDY Club
OPEN MIC NITE
KDOK KDOK KDOK
IN WHAT RELATIONSHIP DO THE COMMUNISTS STAND TO THE PROLETARIANS AS A WHOLE?
THE IMMEDIATE AIM OF THE COMMUNISTS IS THE SAME AS THAT OF ALL THE OTHER PROLETARIAN PARTIES: FORMATION OF THE PROLETARIAT INTO A CLASS, OVERTHROW OF THE BOURGEOIS SUPREMACY, CONQUEST OF POLITICAL POWER BY THE PROLETARIAT!
WC

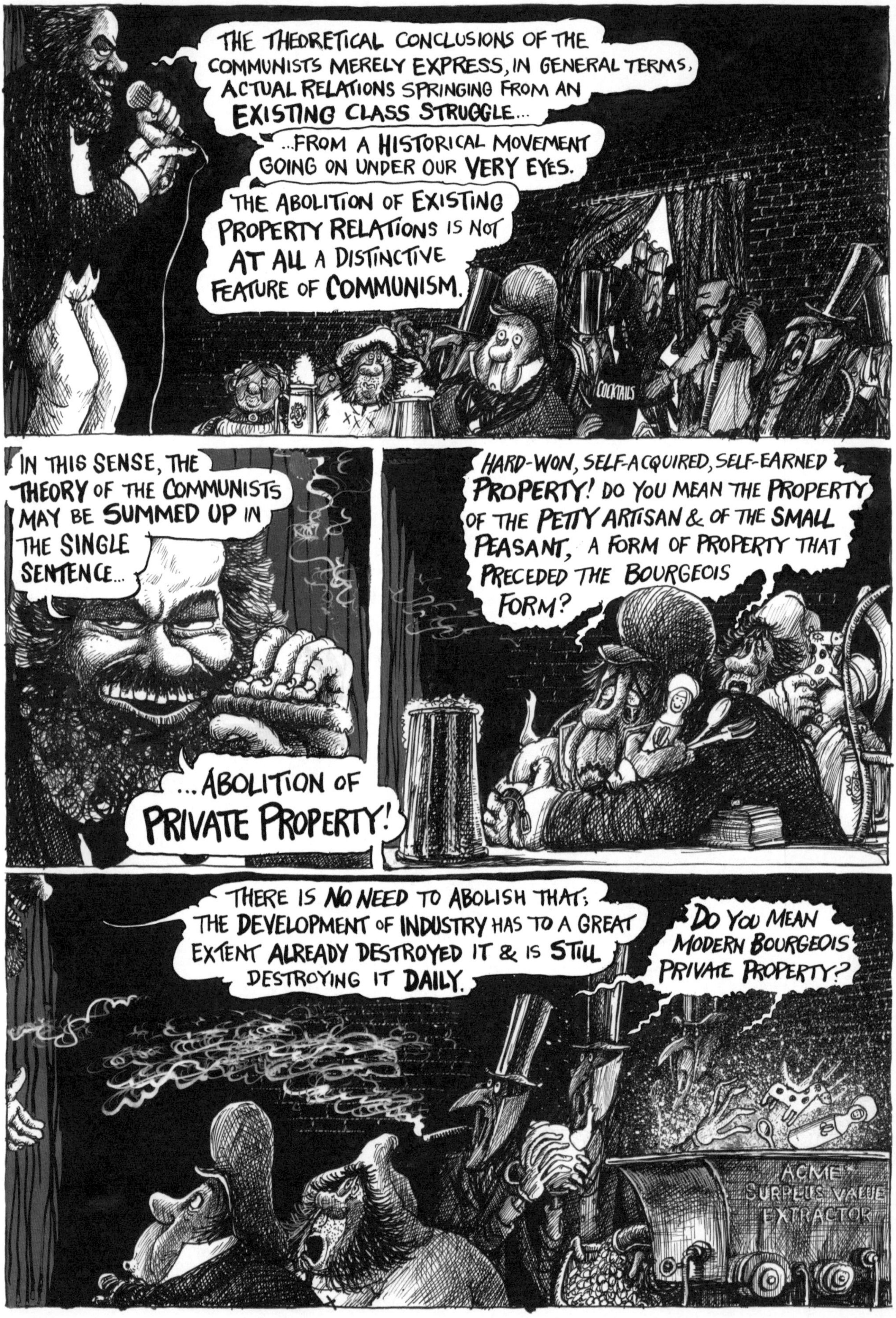

THE THEORETICAL CONCLUSIONS OF THE COMMUNISTS MERELY EXPRESS, IN GENERAL TERMS, ACTUAL RELATIONS SPRINGING FROM AN EXISTING CLASS STRUGGLE...
...FROM A HISTORICAL MOVEMENT GOING ON UNDER OUR VERY EYES.
THE ABOLITION OF EXISTING PROPERTY RELATIONS IS NOT AT ALL A DISTINCTIVE FEATURE OF COMMUNISM.
COCKTAILS
IN THIS SENSE, THE THEORY OF THE COMMUNISTS MAY BE SUMMED UP IN THE SINGLE SENTENCE...
...ABOLITION OF PRIVATE PROPERTY!
HARD-WON, SELF-ACQUIRED, SELF-EARNED PROPERTY! DO YOU MEAN THE PROPERTY OF THE PETTY ARTISAN & OF THE SMALL PEASANT, A FORM OF PROPERTY THAT PRECEDED THE BOURGEOIS FORM?
THERE IS NO NEED TO ABOLISH THAT; THE DEVELOPMENT OF INDUSTRY HAS TO A GREAT EXTENT ALREADY DESTROYED IT & IS STILL DESTROYING IT DAILY.
DO YOU MEAN MODERN BOURGEOIS PRIVATE PROPERTY?
ACME SURPLUS VALUE EXTRACTOR

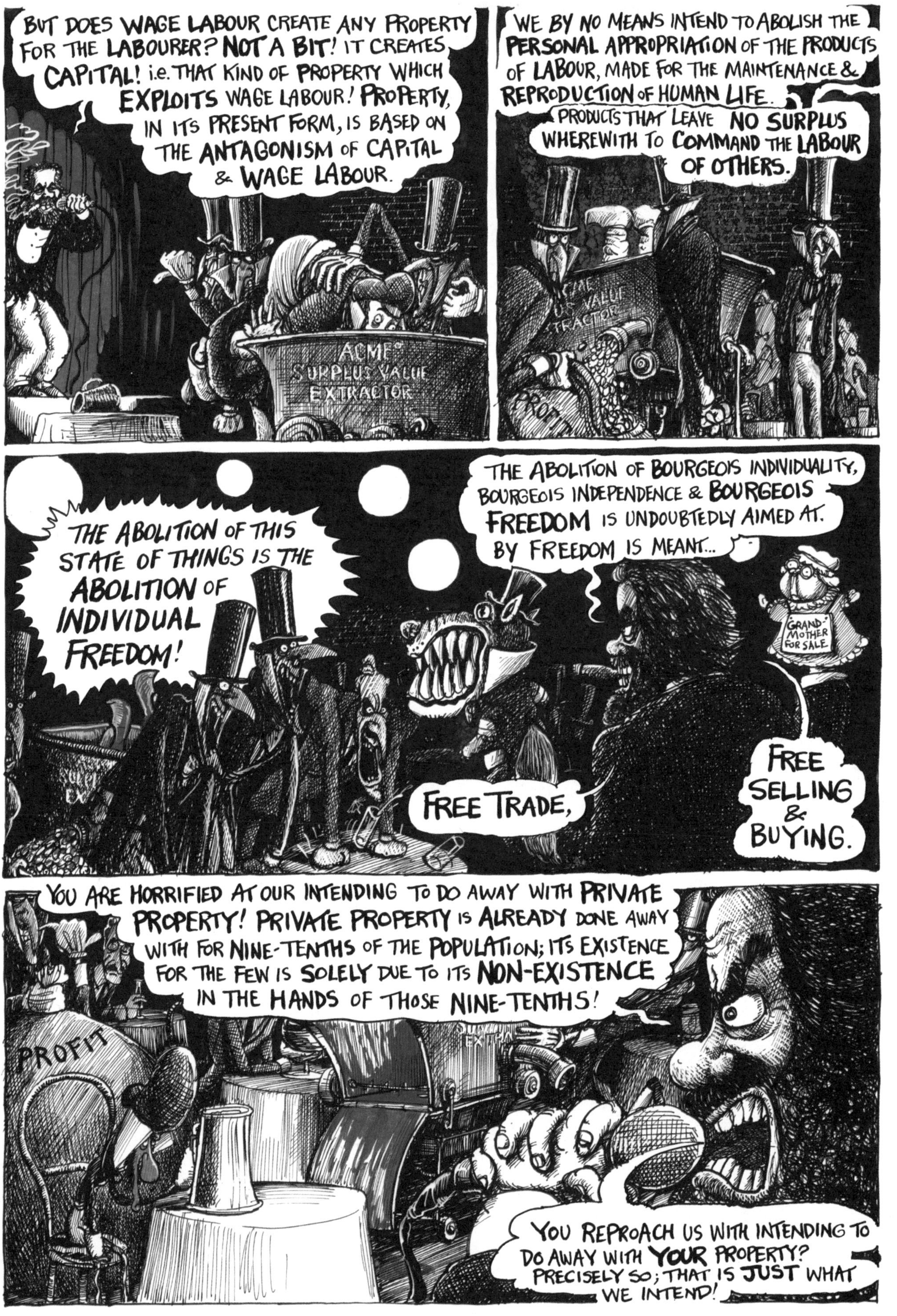
BUT DOES WAGE LABOUR CREATE ANY PROPERTY FOR THE LABOURER? NOT A BIT! IT CREATES CAPITAL! i.e. THAT KIND OF PROPERTY WHICH EXPLOITS WAGE LABOUR! PROPERTY, IN ITS PRESENT FORM, IS BASED ON THE ANTAGONISM OF CAPITAL & WAGE LABOUR.
ACME SURPLUS VALUE EXTRACTOR
WE BY NO MEANS INTEND TO ABOLISH THE PERSONAL APPROPRIATION OF THE PRODUCTS OF LABOUR, MADE FOR THE MAINTENANCE & REPRODUCTION OF HUMAN LIFE.
PRODUCTS THAT LEAVE NO SURPLUS WHEREWITH TO COMMAND THE LABOUR OF OTHERS.
THE ABOLITION OF THIS STATE OF THINGS IS THE ABOLITION OF INDIVIDUAL FREEDOM!
THE ABOLITION OF BOURGEOIS INDIVIDUALITY, BOURGEOIS INDEPENDENCE & BOURGEOIS FREEDOM IS UNDOUBTEDLY AIMED AT. BY FREEDOM IS MEANT...
GRAND-MOTHER FOR SALE
FREE TRADE,
FREE SELLING & BUYING.
YOU ARE HORRIFIED AT OUR INTENDING TO DO AWAY WITH PRIVATE PROPERTY! PRIVATE PROPERTY IS ALREADY DONE AWAY WITH FOR NINE-TENTHS OF THE POPULATION; ITS EXISTENCE FOR THE FEW IS SOLELY DUE TO ITS NON-EXISTENCE IN THE HANDS OF THOSE NINE-TENTHS!
PROFIT
YOU REPROACH US WITH INTENDING TO DO AWAY WITH YOUR PROPERTY? PRECISELY SO; THAT IS JUST WHAT WE INTEND!

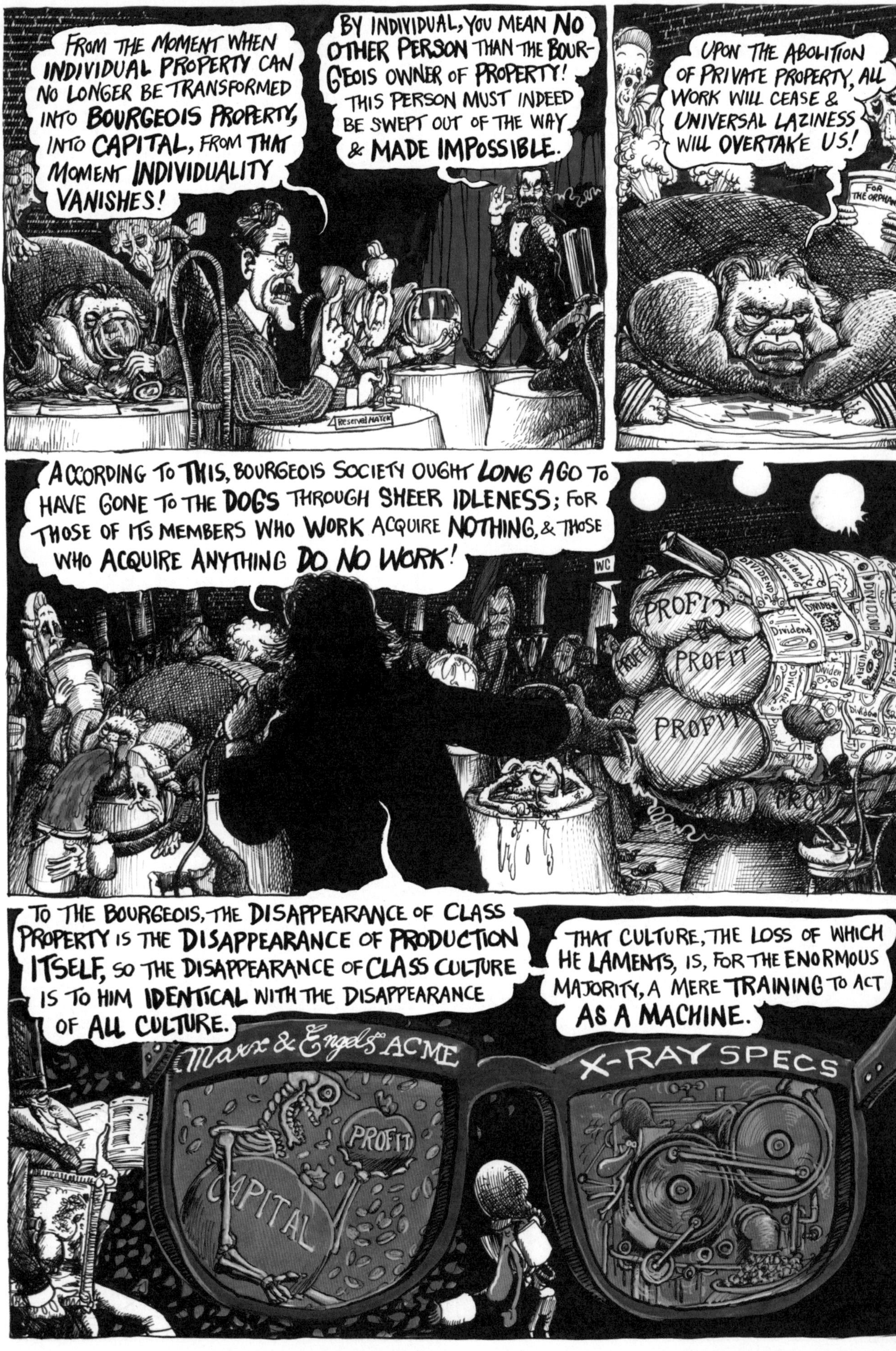
FROM THE MOMENT WHEN INDIVIDUAL PROPERTY CAN NO LONGER BE TRANSFORMED INTO BOURGEOIS PROPERTY, INTO CAPITAL, FROM THAT MOMENT INDIVIDUALITY VANISHES!
BY INDIVIDUAL, YOU MEAN NO OTHER PERSON THAN THE BOURGEOIS OWNER OF PROPERTY! THIS PERSON MUST INDEED BE SWEPT OUT OF THE WAY & MADE IMPOSSIBLE.
Reserved MATEK
UPON THE ABOLITION OF PRIVATE PROPERTY, ALL WORK WILL CEASE & UNIVERSAL LAZINESS WILL OVERTAKE US!
FOR THE ORPHANS
ACCORDING TO THIS, BOURGEOIS SOCIETY OUGHT LONG AGO TO HAVE GONE TO THE DOGS THROUGH SHEER IDLENESS; FOR THOSE OF ITS MEMBERS WHO WORK ACQUIRE NOTHING, & THOSE WHO ACQUIRE ANYTHING DO NO WORK!
WC
PROFIT
PROFIT
PROFIT
Dividend
TO THE BOURGEOIS, THE DISAPPEARANCE OF CLASS PROPERTY IS THE DISAPPEARANCE OF PRODUCTION ITSELF, SO THE DISAPPEARANCE OF CLASS CULTURE IS TO HIM IDENTICAL WITH THE DISAPPEARANCE OF ALL CULTURE.
THAT CULTURE, THE LOSS OF WHICH HE LAMENTS, IS, FOR THE ENORMOUS MAJORITY, A MERE TRAINING TO ACT AS A MACHINE.
Marx & Engels ACME X-RAY SPECS
PROFIT
CAPITAL

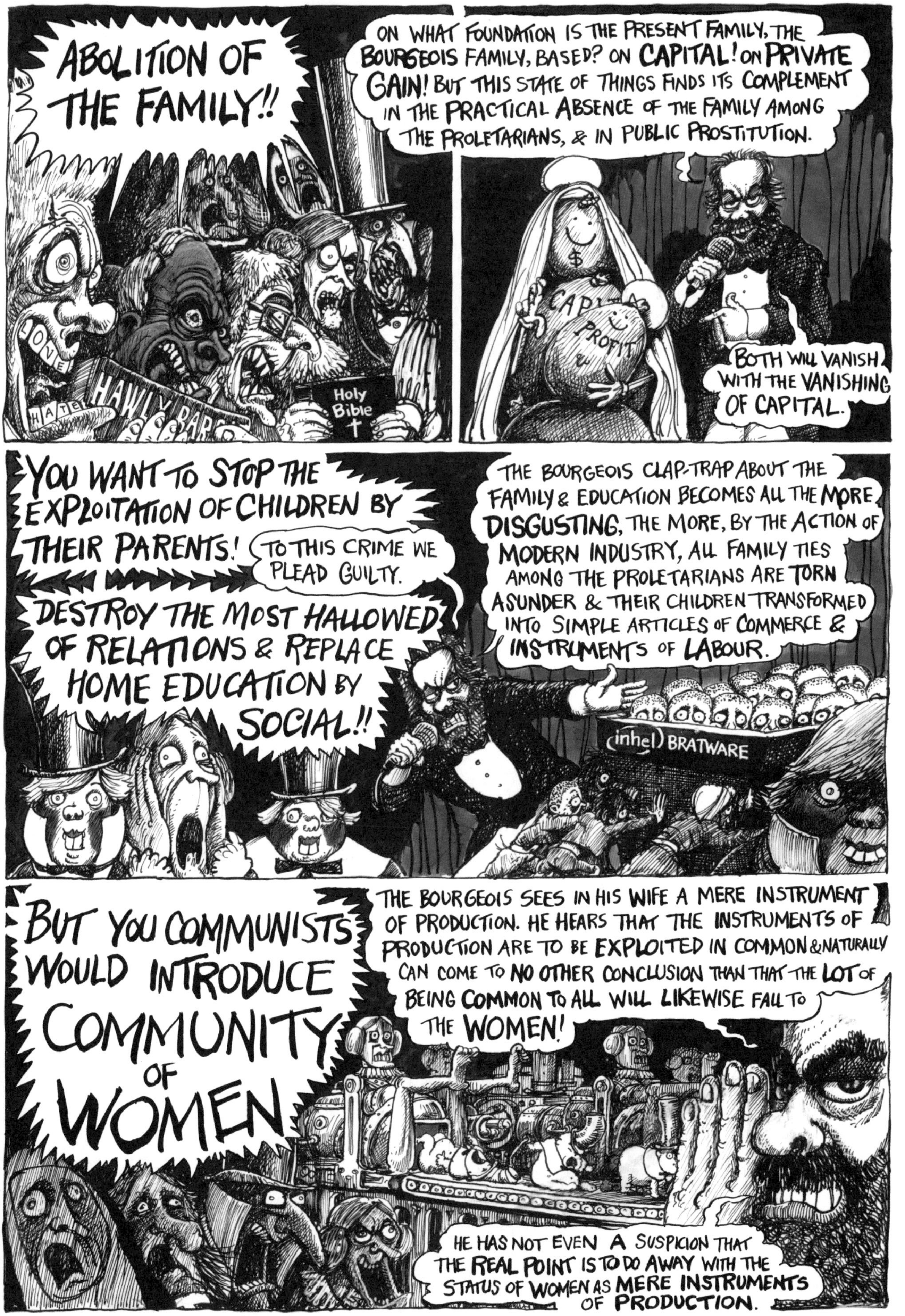
ABOLITION OF THE FAMILY!!
ON WHAT FOUNDATION IS THE PRESENT FAMILY, THE BOURGEOIS FAMILY, BASED? ON CAPITAL! ON PRIVATE GAIN! BUT THIS STATE OF THINGS FINDS ITS COMPLEMENT IN THE PRACTICAL ABSENCE OF THE FAMILY AMONG THE PROLETARIANS, & IN PUBLIC PROSTITUTION.
LOVE
HATE
HAWLY BARS
Holy Bible
PROFIT
BOTH WILL VANISH WITH THE VANISHING OF CAPITAL.
YOU WANT TO STOP THE EXPLOITATION OF CHILDREN BY THEIR PARENTS!
TO THIS CRIME WE PLEAD GUILTY.
DESTROY THE MOST HALLOWED OF RELATIONS & REPLACE HOME EDUCATION BY SOCIAL!!
THE BOURGEOIS CLAP-TRAP ABOUT THE FAMILY & EDUCATION BECOMES ALL THE MORE DISGUSTING, THE MORE, BY THE ACTION OF MODERN INDUSTRY, ALL FAMILY TIES AMONG THE PROLETARIANS ARE TORN ASUNDER & THEIR CHILDREN TRANSFORMED INTO SIMPLE ARTICLES OF COMMERCE & INSTRUMENTS OF LABOUR.
(inhel) BRATWARE
BUT YOU COMMUNISTS WOULD INTRODUCE COMMUNITY OF WOMEN
THE BOURGEOIS SEES IN HIS WIFE A MERE INSTRUMENT OF PRODUCTION. HE HEARS THAT THE INSTRUMENTS OF PRODUCTION ARE TO BE EXPLOITED IN COMMON & NATURALLY CAN COME TO NO OTHER CONCLUSION THAN THAT THE LOT OF BEING COMMON TO ALL WILL LIKEWISE FALL TO THE WOMEN!
HE HAS NOT EVEN A SUSPICION THAT THE REAL POINT IS TO DO AWAY WITH THE STATUS OF WOMEN AS MERE INSTRUMENTS OF PRODUCTION.

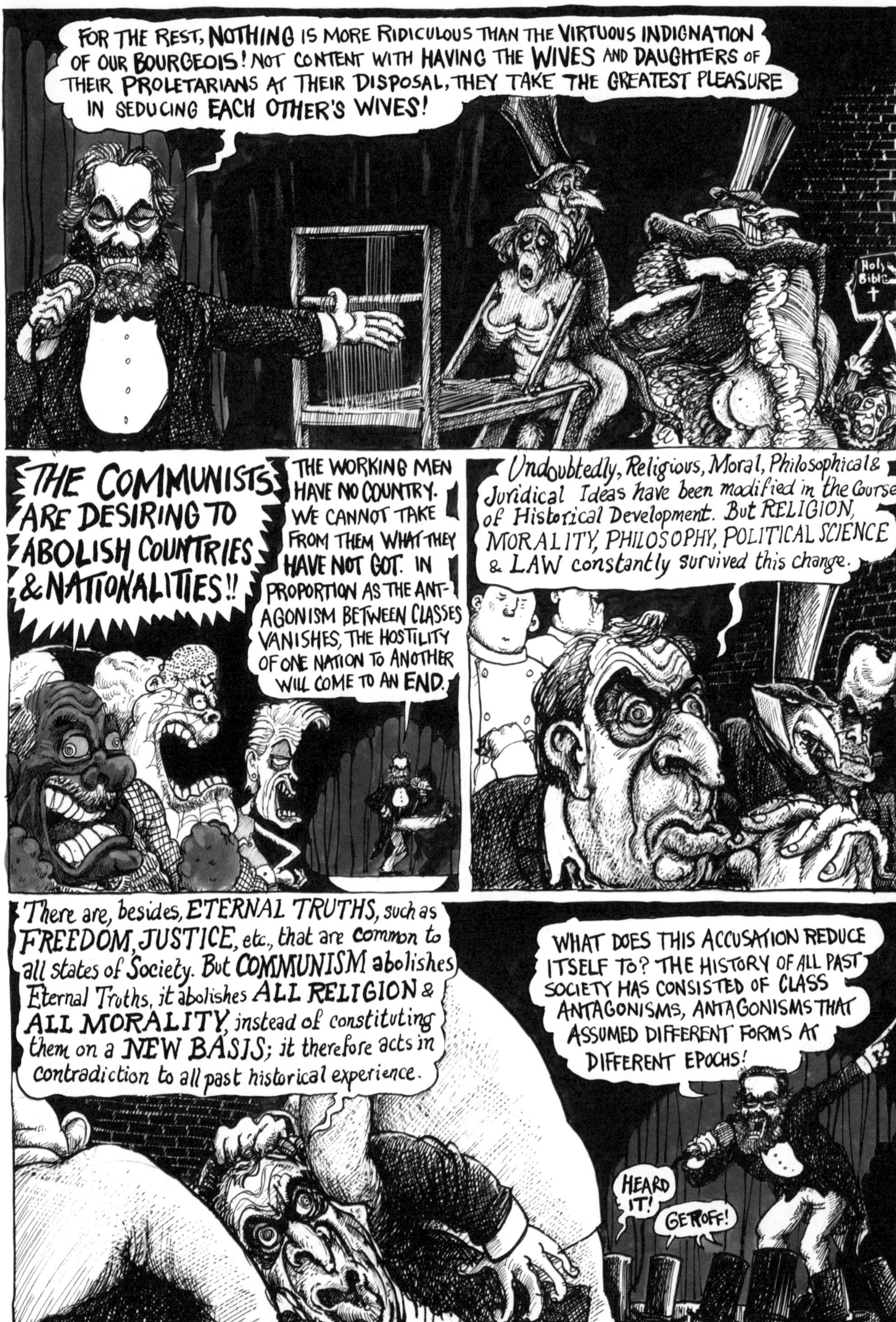
FOR THE REST, NOTHING IS MORE RIDICULOUS THAN THE VIRTUOUS INDIGNATION OF OUR BOURGEOIS! NOT CONTENT WITH HAVING THE WIVES AND DAUGHTERS OF THEIR PROLETARIANS AT THEIR DISPOSAL, THEY TAKE THE GREATEST PLEASURE IN SEDUCING EACH OTHER'S WIVES!
Holy Bible
THE COMMUNISTS ARE DESIRING TO ABOLISH COUNTRIES & NATIONALITIES!!
THE WORKING MEN HAVE NO COUNTRY. WE CANNOT TAKE FROM THEM WHAT THEY HAVE NOT GOT. IN PROPORTION AS THE ANTAGONISM BETWEEN CLASSES VANISHES, THE HOSTILITY OF ONE NATION TO ANOTHER WILL COME TO AN END.
Undoubtedly, Religious, Moral, Philosophical & Juridical Ideas have been modified in the Course of Historical Development. But RELIGION, MORALITY, PHILOSOPHY, POLITICAL SCIENCE & LAW constantly survived this change.
There are, besides, ETERNAL TRUTHS, such as FREEDOM, JUSTICE, etc., that are common to all states of Society. But COMMUNISM abolishes Eternal Truths, it abolishes ALL RELIGION & ALL MORALITY, instead of constituting them on a NEW BASIS; it therefore acts in contradiction to all past historical experience.
WHAT DOES THIS ACCUSATION REDUCE ITSELF TO? THE HISTORY OF ALL PAST SOCIETY HAS CONSISTED OF CLASS ANTAGONISMS, ANTAGONISMS THAT ASSUMED DIFFERENT FORMS AT DIFFERENT EPOCHS!
HEARD IT!
GETROFF!

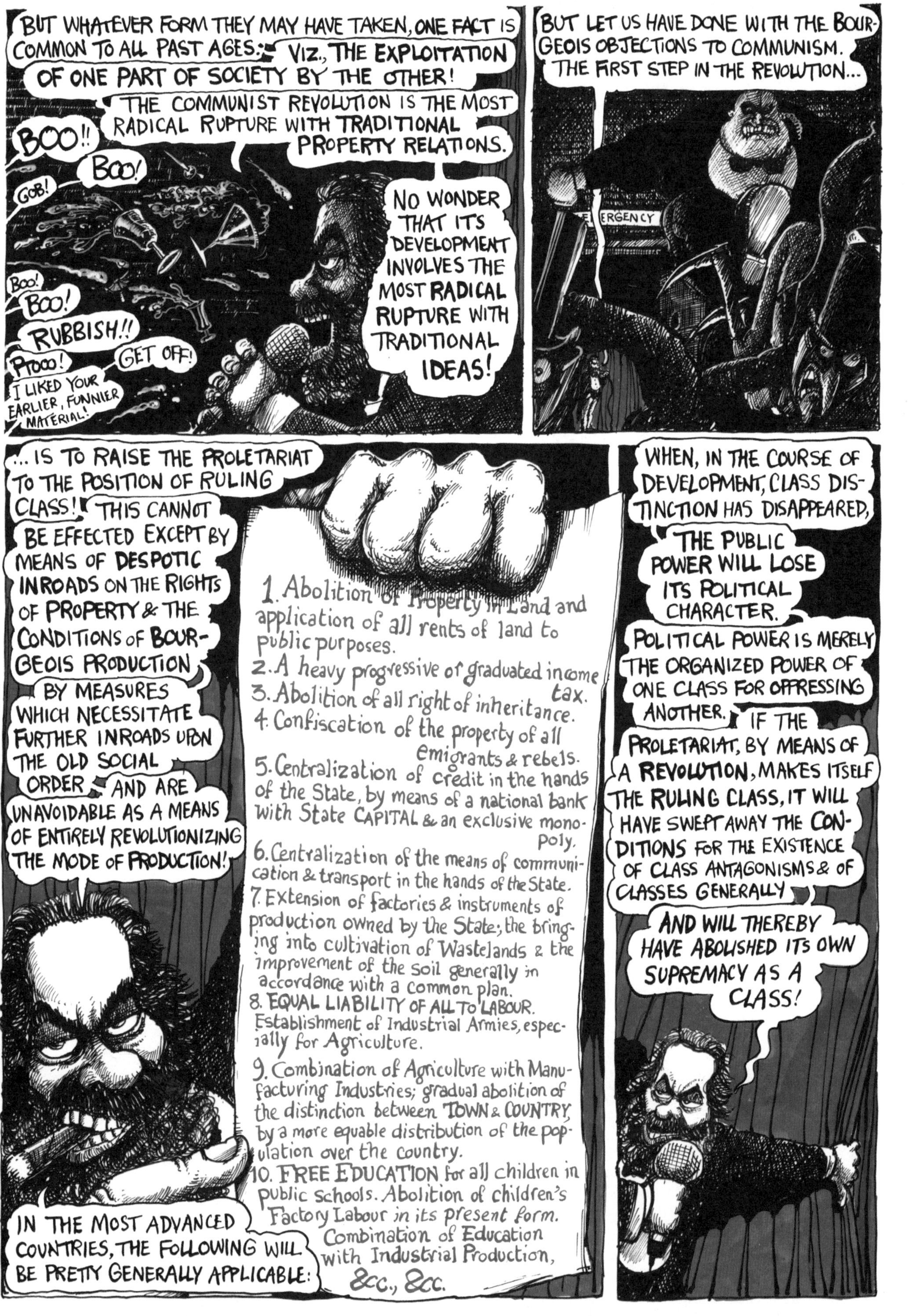
BUT WHATEVER FORM THEY MAY HAVE TAKEN, ONE FACT IS COMMON TO ALL PAST AGES:
VIZ., THE EXPLOITATION OF ONE PART OF SOCIETY BY THE OTHER!
THE COMMUNIST REVOLUTION IS THE MOST RADICAL RUPTURE WITH TRADITIONAL PROPERTY RELATIONS.
BOO!!
BOO!
GOB!
NO WONDER THAT ITS DEVELOPMENT INVOLVES THE MOST RADICAL RUPTURE WITH TRADITIONAL IDEAS!
Boo!
BOO!
RUBBISH!!
Prooo!
GET OFF!
I LIKED YOUR EARLIER, FUNNIER MATERIAL!
BUT LET US HAVE DONE WITH THE BOURGEOIS OBJECTIONS TO COMMUNISM. THE FIRST STEP IN THE REVOLUTION...
ERGENCY
...IS TO RAISE THE PROLETARIAT TO THE POSITION OF RULING CLASS!
THIS CANNOT BE EFFECTED EXCEPT BY MEANS OF DESPOTIC INROADS ON THE RIGHTS OF PROPERTY & THE CONDITIONS OF BOURGEOIS PRODUCTION
BY MEASURES WHICH NECESSITATE FURTHER INROADS UPON THE OLD SOCIAL ORDER
AND ARE UNAVOIDABLE AS A MEANS OF ENTIRELY REVOLUTIONIZING THE MODE OF PRODUCTION!
IN THE MOST ADVANCED COUNTRIES, THE FOLLOWING WILL BE PRETTY GENERALLY APPLICABLE:
1. Abolition of Property in Land and application of all rents of land to public purposes.
2. A heavy progressive or graduated income tax.
3. Abolition of all right of inheritance.
4. Confiscation of the property of all emigrants & rebels.
5. Centralization of credit in the hands of the State, by means of a national bank with State CAPITAL & an exclusive monopoly.
6. Centralization of the means of communication & transport in the hands of the State.
7. Extension of factories & instruments of production owned by the State; the bringing into cultivation of Wastelands & the improvement of the soil generally in accordance with a common plan.
8. EQUAL LIABILITY OF ALL TO LABOUR. Establishment of Industrial Armies, especially for Agriculture.
9. Combination of Agriculture with Manufacturing Industries; gradual abolition of the distinction between TOWN & COUNTRY, by a more equable distribution of the population over the country.
10. FREE EDUCATION for all children in public schools. Abolition of children's Factory Labour in its present form. Combination of Education with Industrial Production, &c., &c.
WHEN, IN THE COURSE OF DEVELOPMENT, CLASS DISTINCTION HAS DISAPPEARED,
THE PUBLIC POWER WILL LOSE ITS POLITICAL CHARACTER.
POLITICAL POWER IS MERELY THE ORGANIZED POWER OF ONE CLASS FOR OPPRESSING ANOTHER.
IF THE PROLETARIAT, BY MEANS OF A REVOLUTION, MAKES ITSELF THE RULING CLASS, IT WILL HAVE SWEPT AWAY THE CONDITIONS FOR THE EXISTENCE OF CLASS ANTAGONISMS & OF CLASSES GENERALLY
AND WILL THEREBY HAVE ABOLISHED ITS OWN SUPREMACY AS A CLASS!

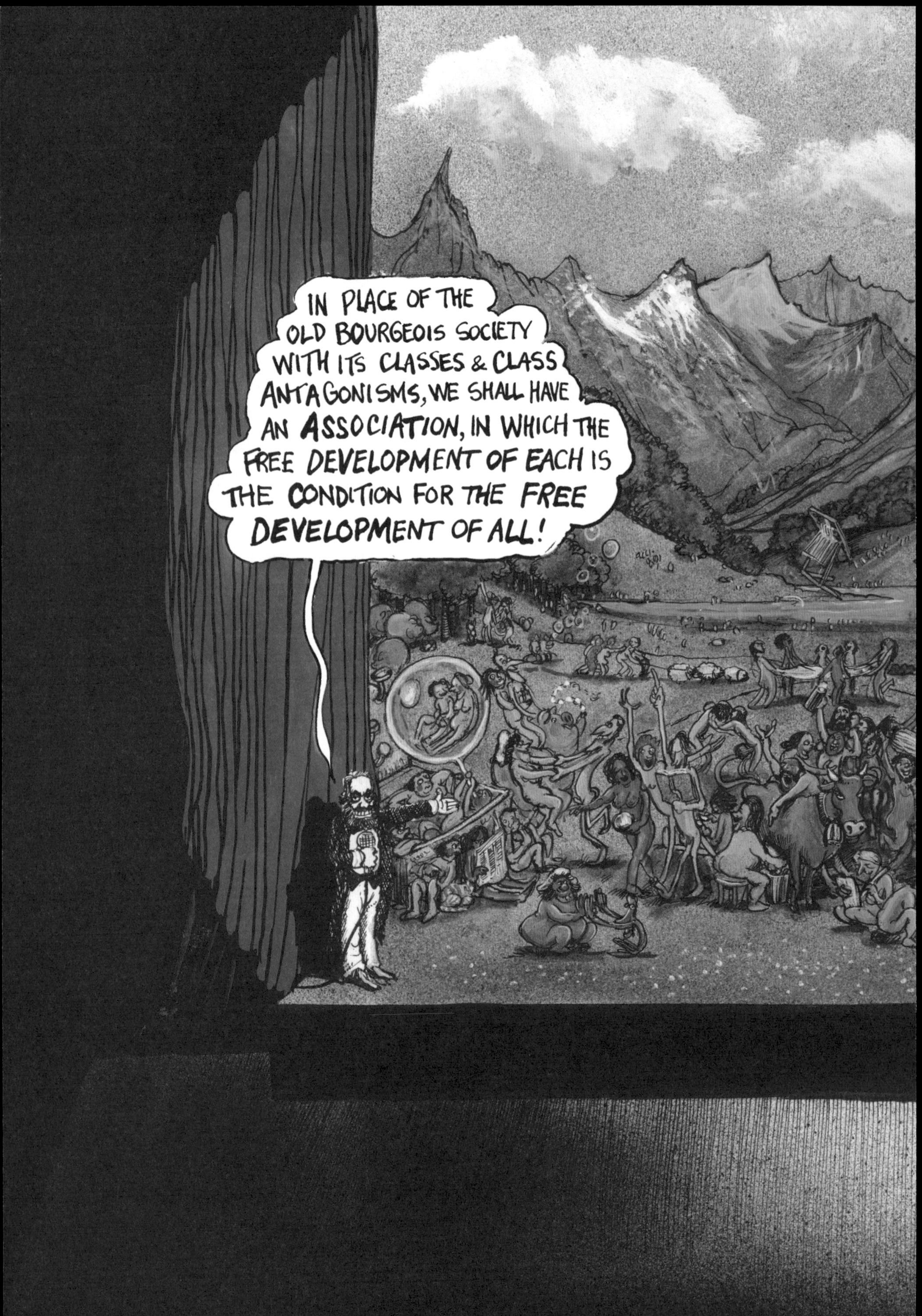
IN PLACE OF THE OLD BOURGEOIS SOCIETY WITH ITS CLASSES & CLASS ANTAGONISMS, WE SHALL HAVE AN ASSOCIATION, IN WHICH THE FREE DEVELOPMENT OF EACH IS THE CONDITION FOR THE FREE DEVELOPMENT OF ALL!

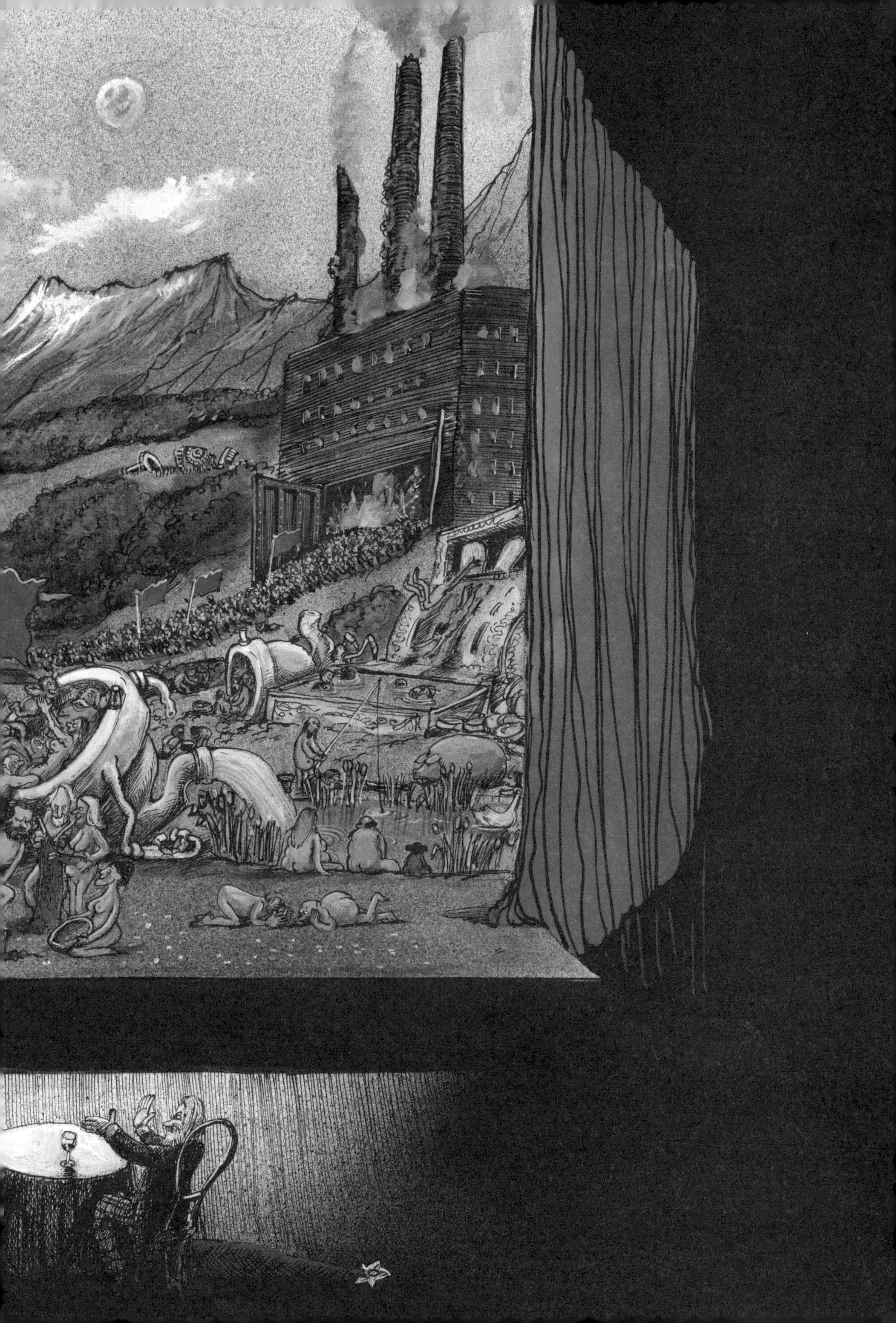

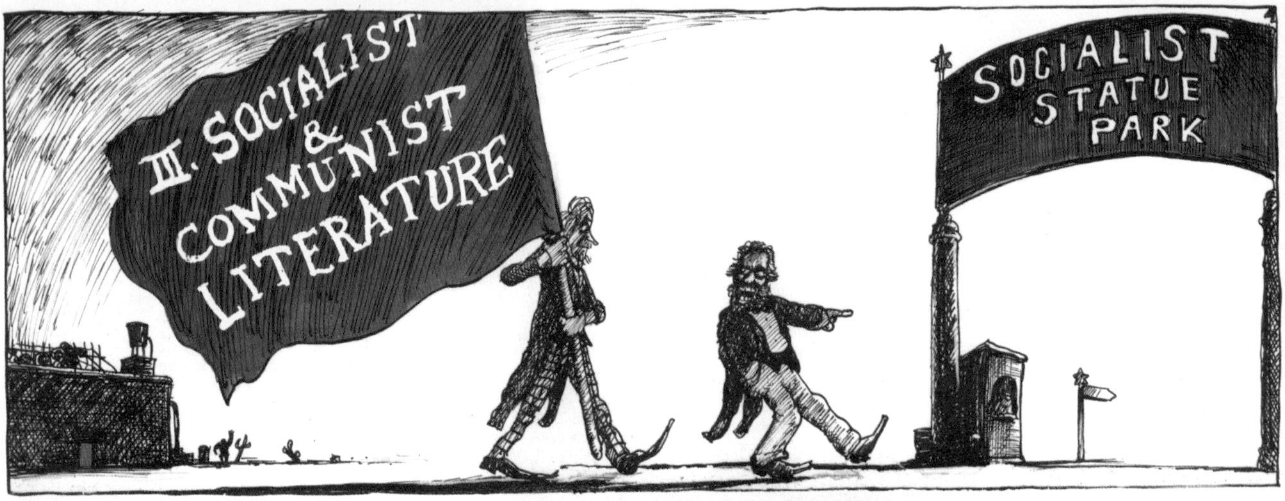
III. SOCIALIST & COMMUNIST LITERATURE
SOCIALIST STATUE PARK

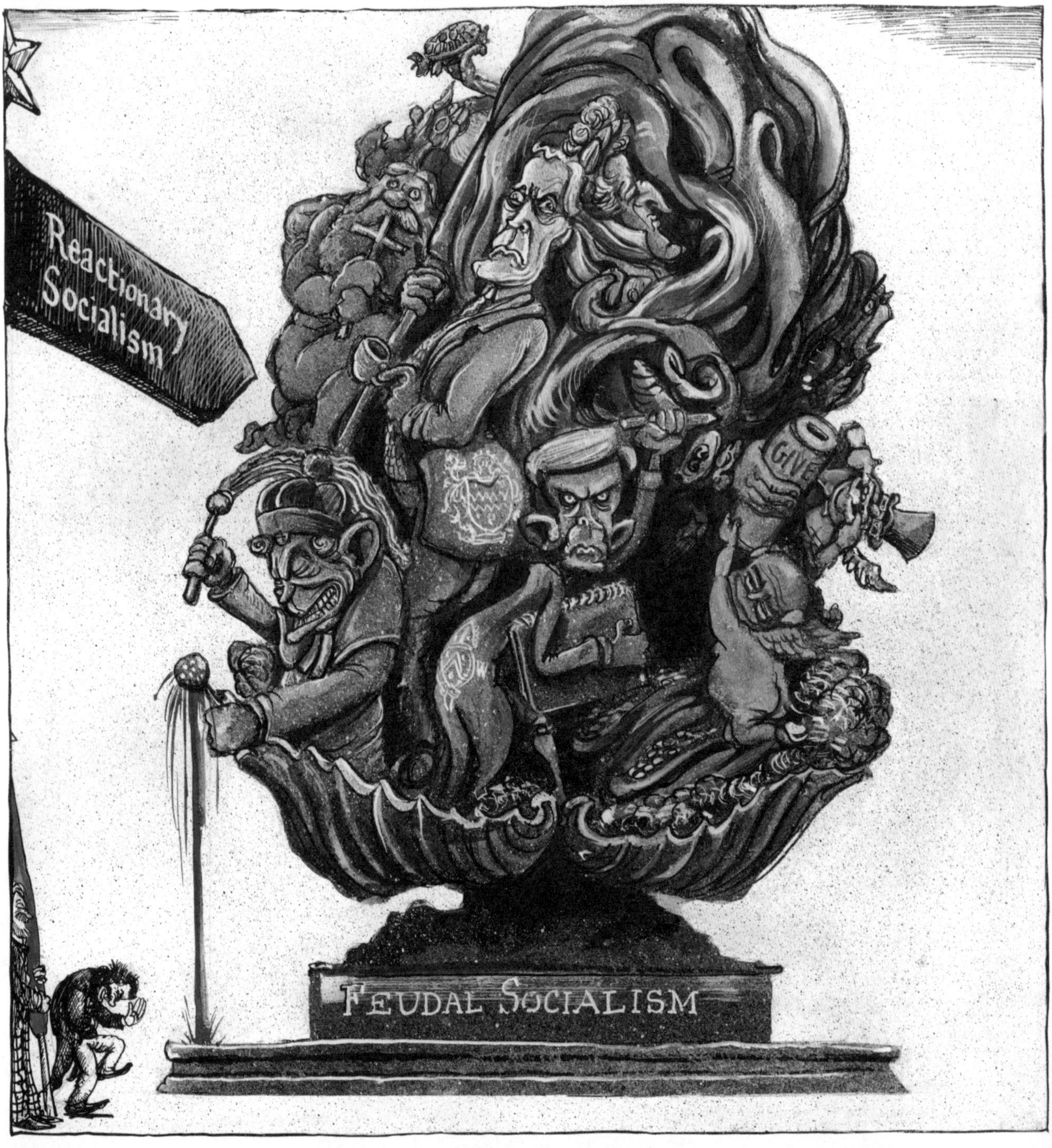
Reactionary Socialism
GIVE
FEUDAL SOCIALISM

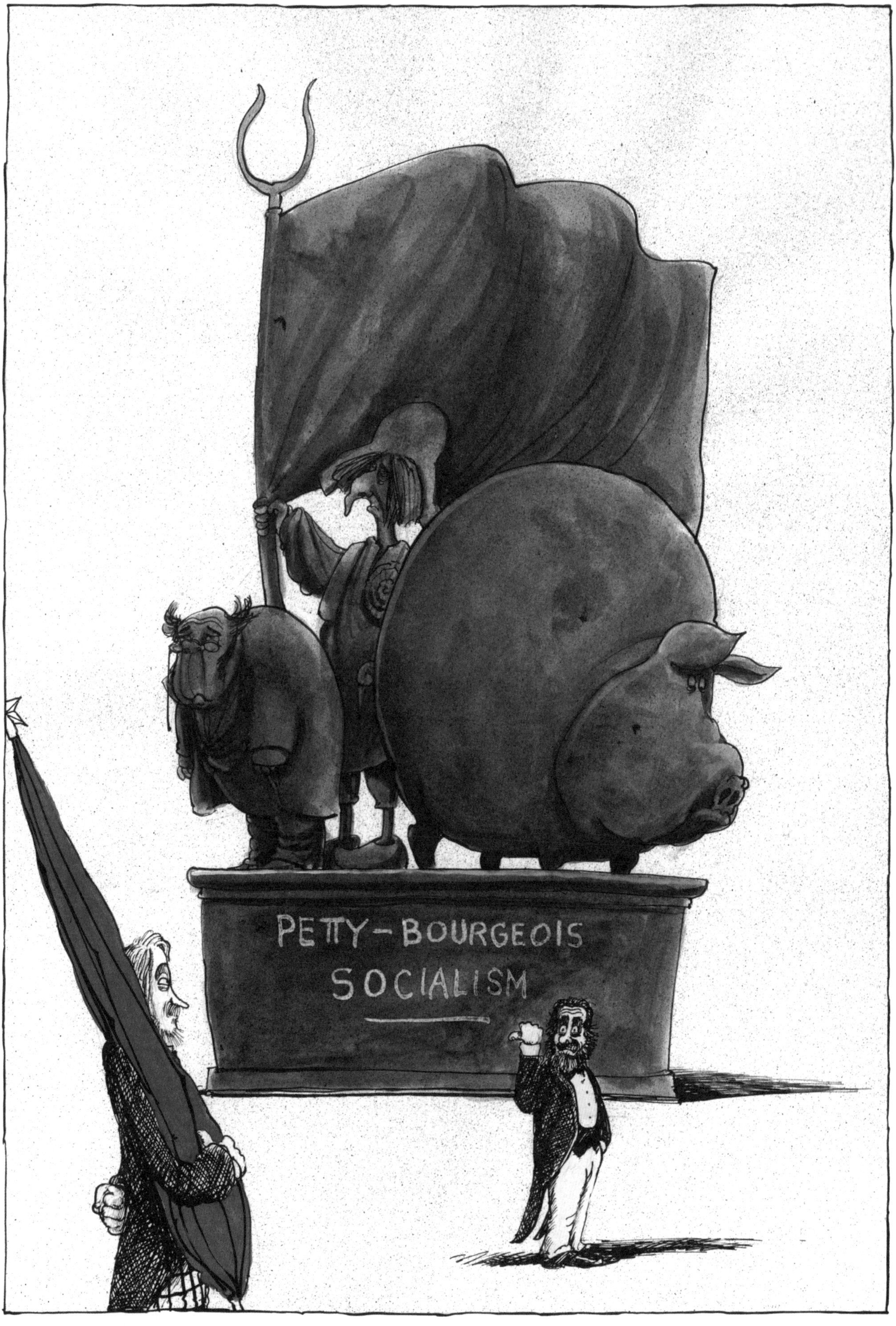
PETTY-BOURGEOIS
SOCIALISM

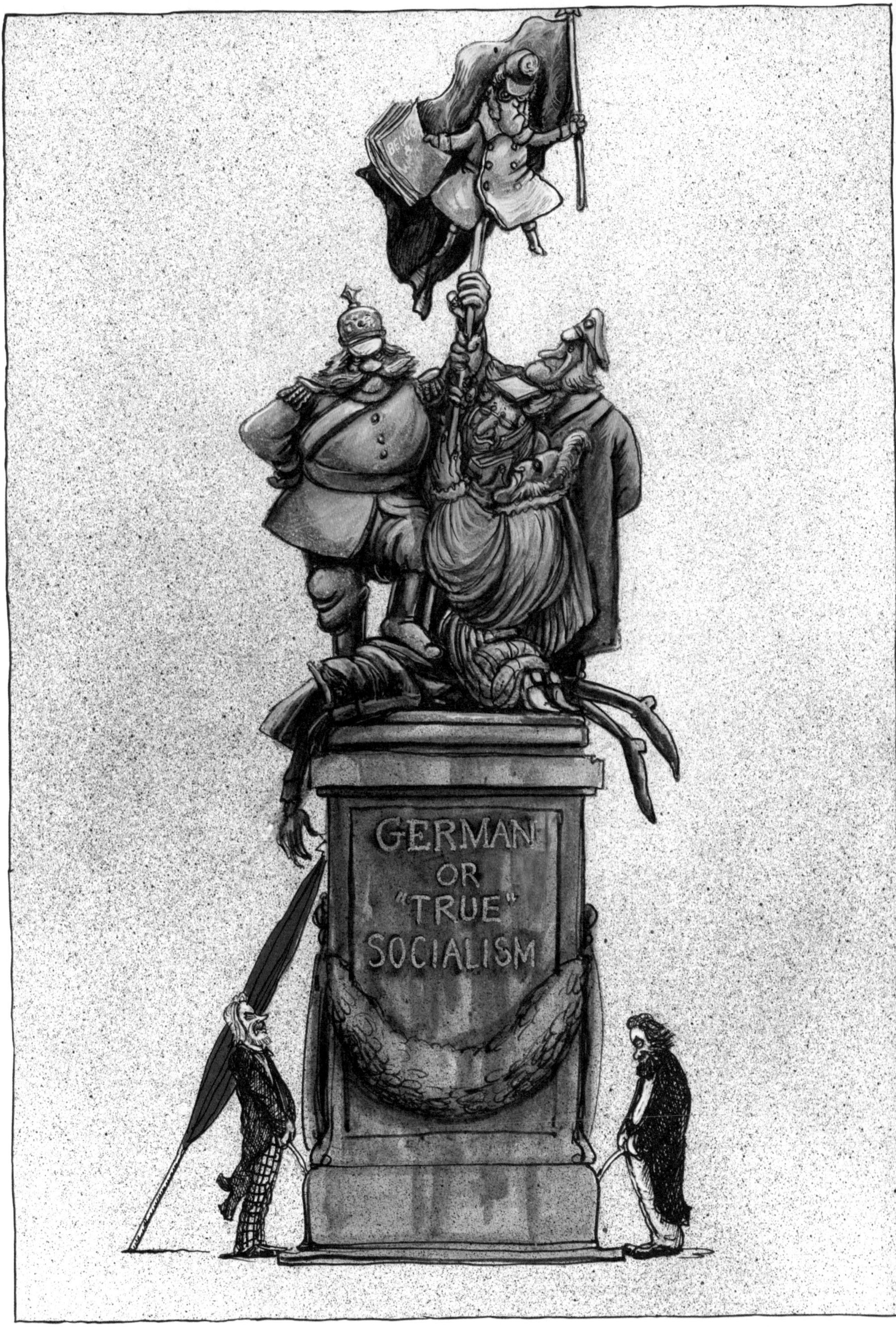
GERMAN
OR
"TRUE"
SOCIALISM

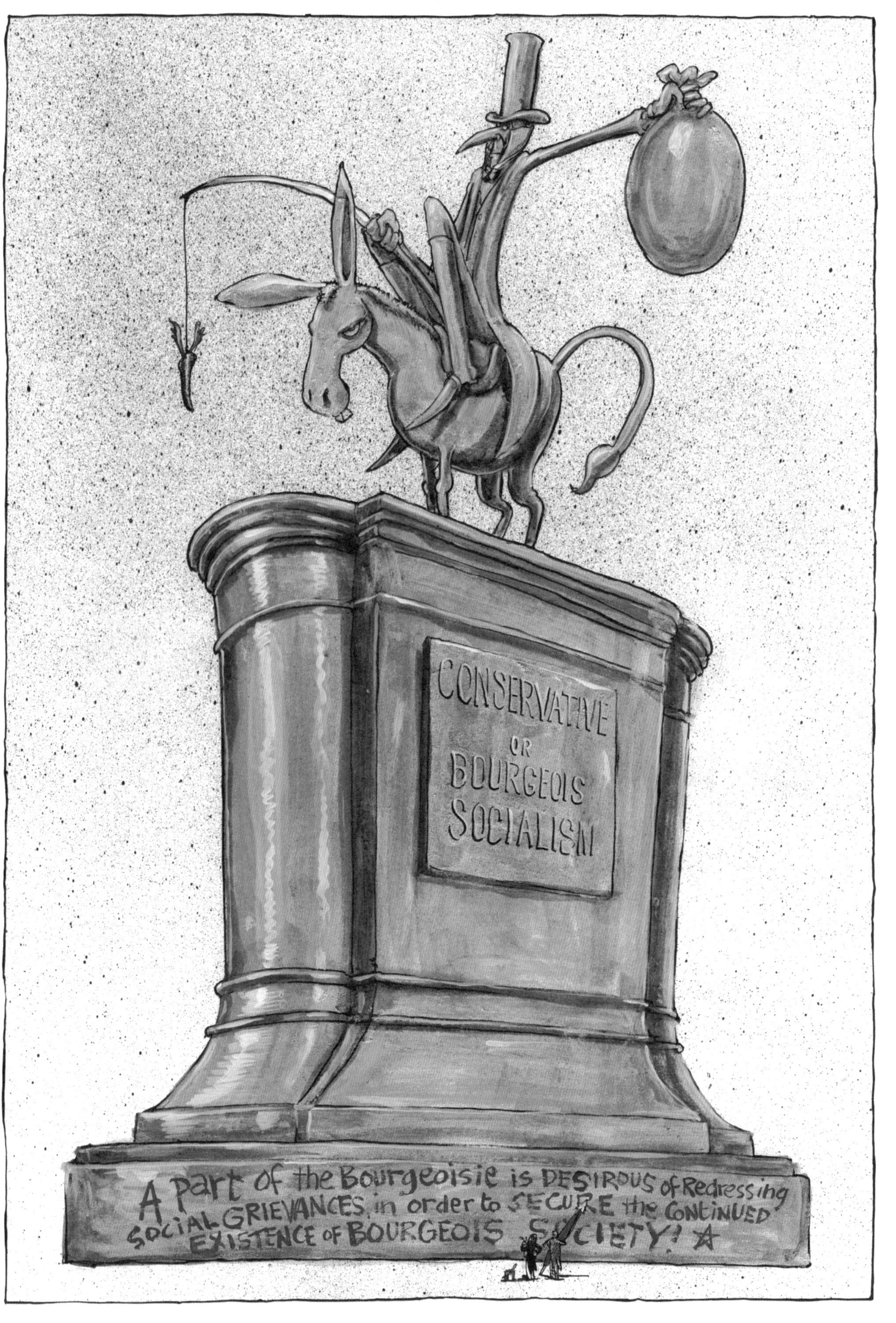
CONSERVATIVE
OR
BOURGEOIS
SOCIALISM
A part of the Bourgeoisie is DESIROUS of Redressing
SOCIAL GRIEVANCES, in order to SECURE the CONTINUED
EXISTENCE OF BOURGEOIS SOCIETY!

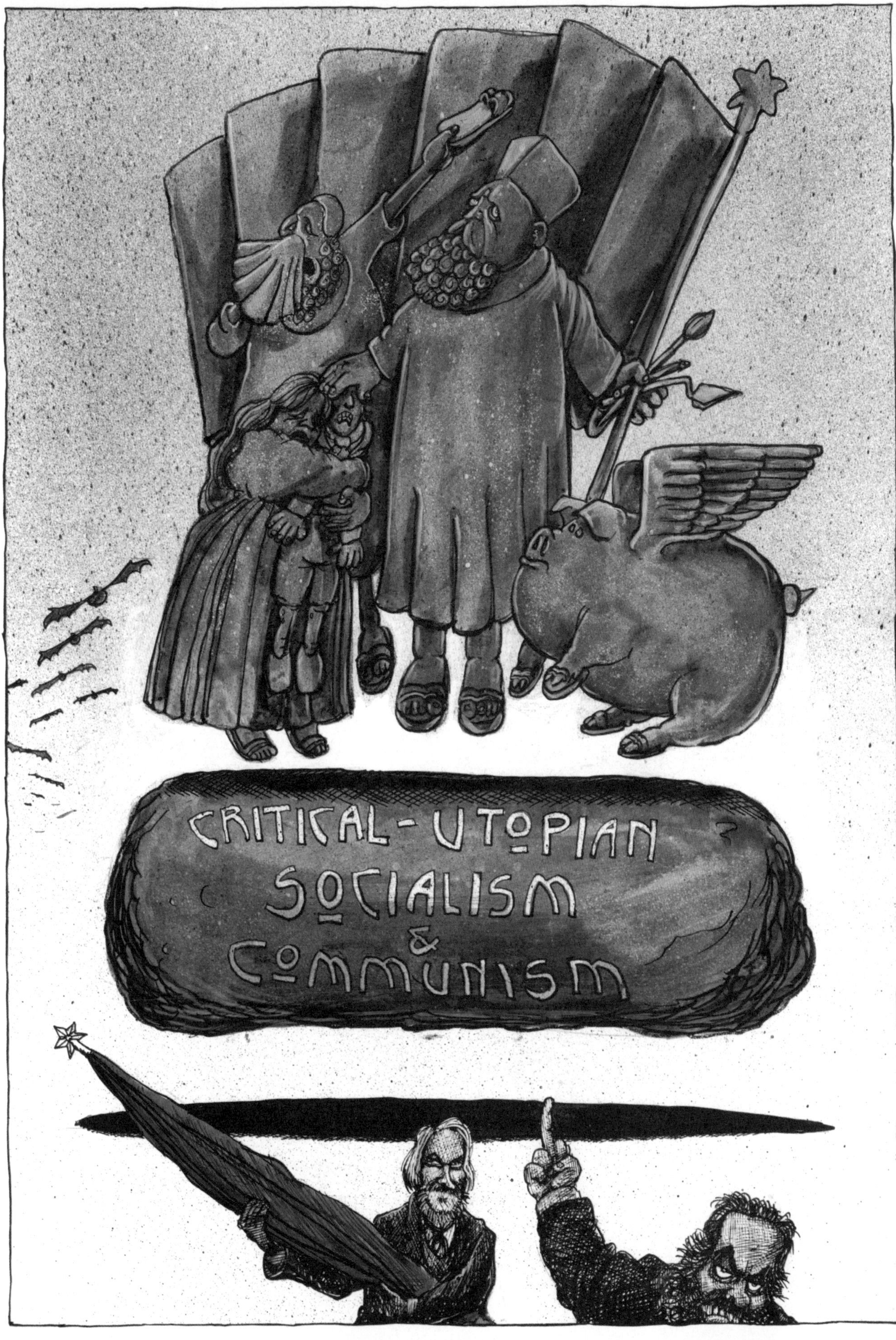
CRITICAL-UTOPIAN
SOCIALISM
&
COMMUNISM

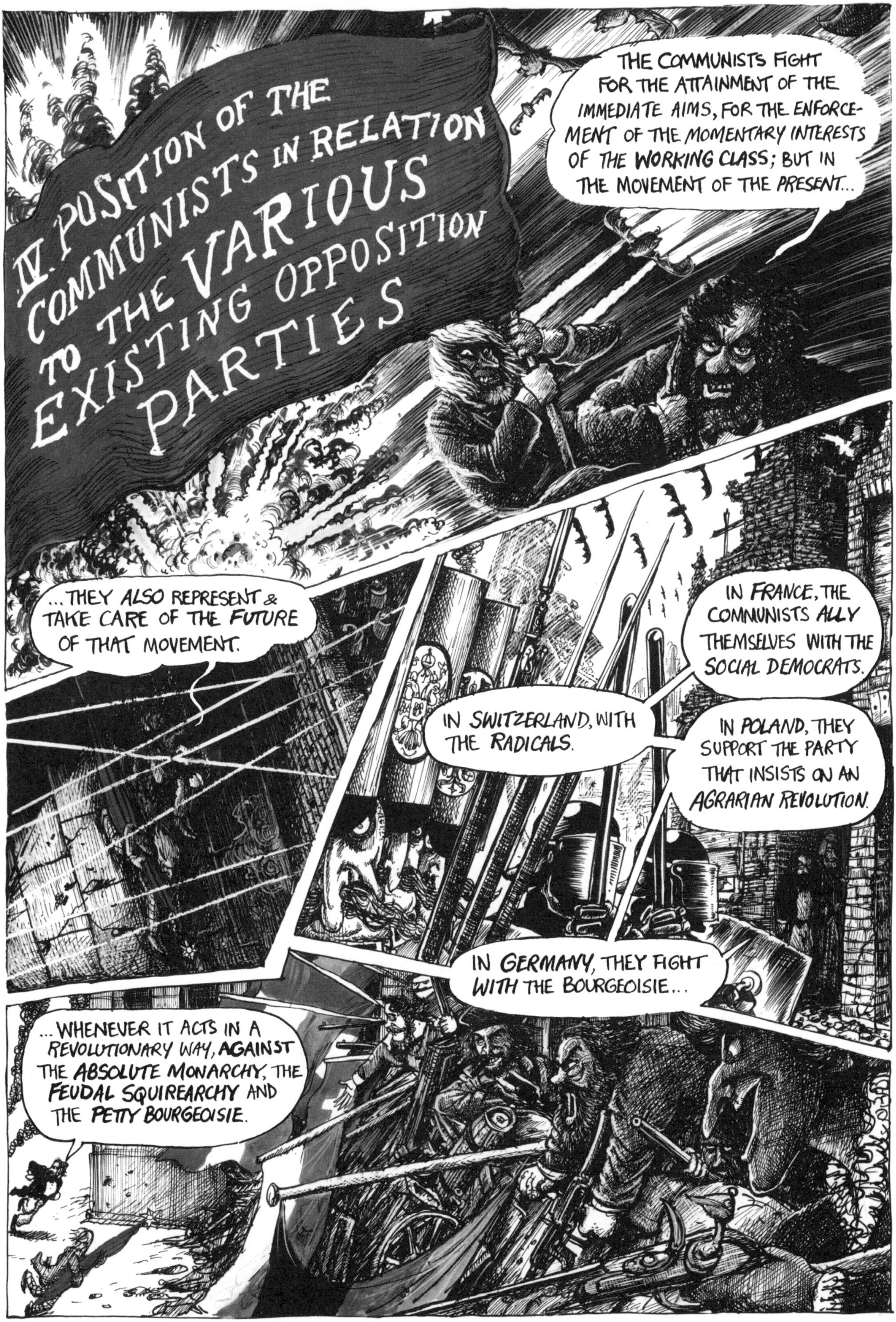
IV. POSITION OF THE COMMUNISTS IN RELATION TO THE VARIOUS EXISTING OPPOSITION PARTIES
THE COMMUNISTS FIGHT FOR THE ATTAINMENT OF THE IMMEDIATE AIMS, FOR THE ENFORCEMENT OF THE MOMENTARY INTERESTS OF THE WORKING CLASS; BUT IN THE MOVEMENT OF THE PRESENT...
...THEY ALSO REPRESENT & TAKE CARE OF THE FUTURE OF THAT MOVEMENT.
IN FRANCE, THE COMMUNISTS ALLY THEMSELVES WITH THE SOCIAL DEMOCRATS.
IN SWITZERLAND, WITH THE RADICALS.
IN POLAND, THEY SUPPORT THE PARTY THAT INSISTS ON AN AGRARIAN REVOLUTION.
IN GERMANY, THEY FIGHT WITH THE BOURGEOISIE...
...WHENEVER IT ACTS IN A REVOLUTIONARY WAY, AGAINST THE ABSOLUTE MONARCHY, THE FEUDAL SQUIREARCHY AND THE PETTY BOURGEOISIE.

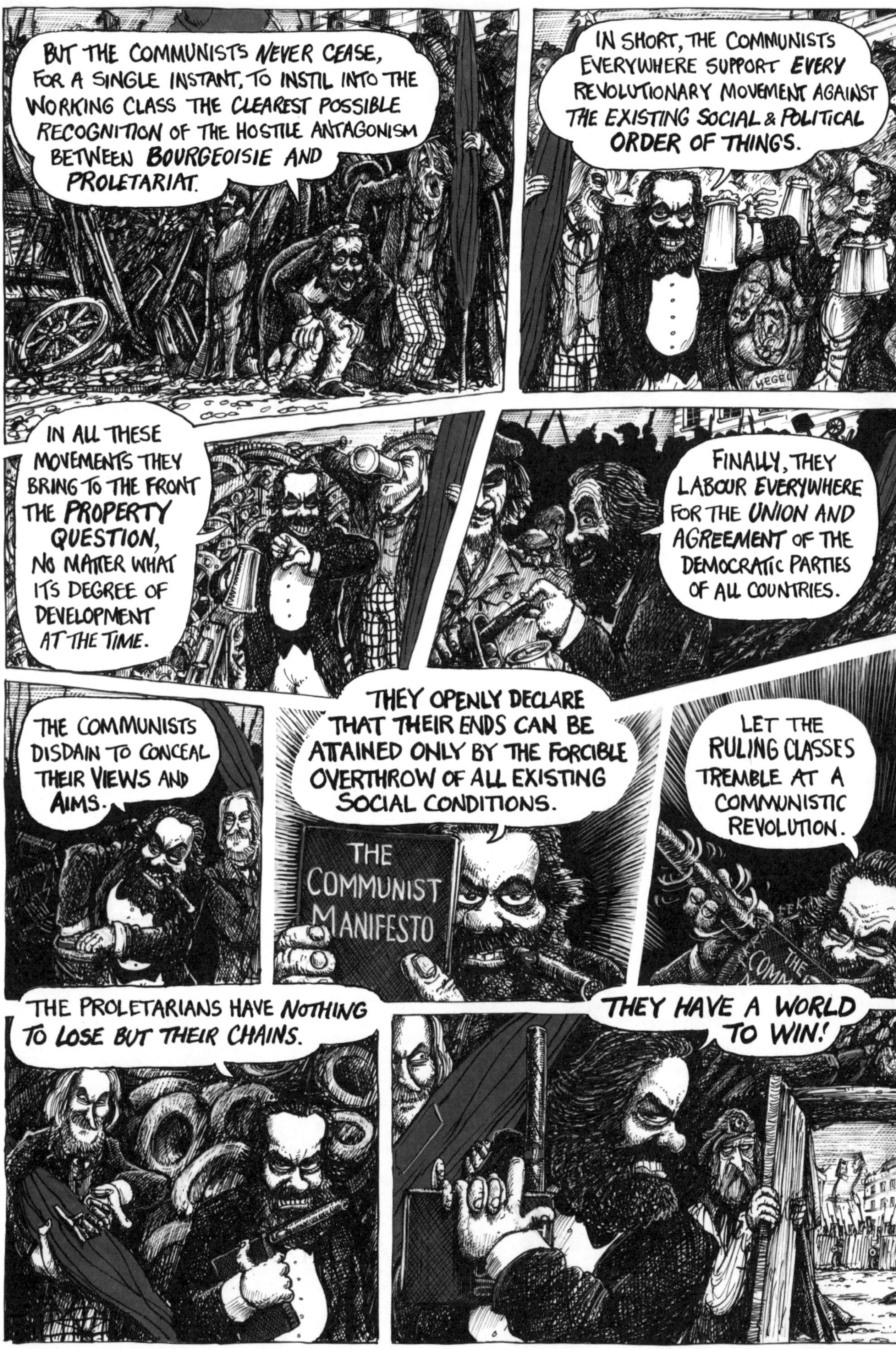
BUT THE COMMUNISTS NEVER CEASE, FOR A SINGLE INSTANT, TO INSTIL INTO THE WORKING CLASS THE CLEAREST POSSIBLE RECOGNITION OF THE HOSTILE ANTAGONISM BETWEEN BOURGEOISIE AND PROLETARIAT.
IN SHORT, THE COMMUNISTS EVERYWHERE SUPPORT EVERY REVOLUTIONARY MOVEMENT AGAINST THE EXISTING SOCIAL & POLITICAL ORDER OF THINGS.
HEGEL
IN ALL THESE MOVEMENTS THEY BRING TO THE FRONT THE PROPERTY QUESTION, NO MATTER WHAT ITS DEGREE OF DEVELOPMENT AT THE TIME.
FINALLY, THEY LABOUR EVERYWHERE FOR THE UNION AND AGREEMENT OF THE DEMOCRATIC PARTIES OF ALL COUNTRIES.
THE COMMUNISTS DISDAIN TO CONCEAL THEIR VIEWS AND AIMS.
THEY OPENLY DECLARE THAT THEIR ENDS CAN BE ATTAINED ONLY BY THE FORCIBLE OVERTHROW OF ALL EXISTING SOCIAL CONDITIONS.
THE COMMUNIST MANIFESTO
LET THE RULING CLASSES TREMBLE AT A COMMUNISTIC REVOLUTION.
THE PROLETARIANS HAVE NOTHING TO LOSE BUT THEIR CHAINS.
THEY HAVE A WORLD TO WIN!

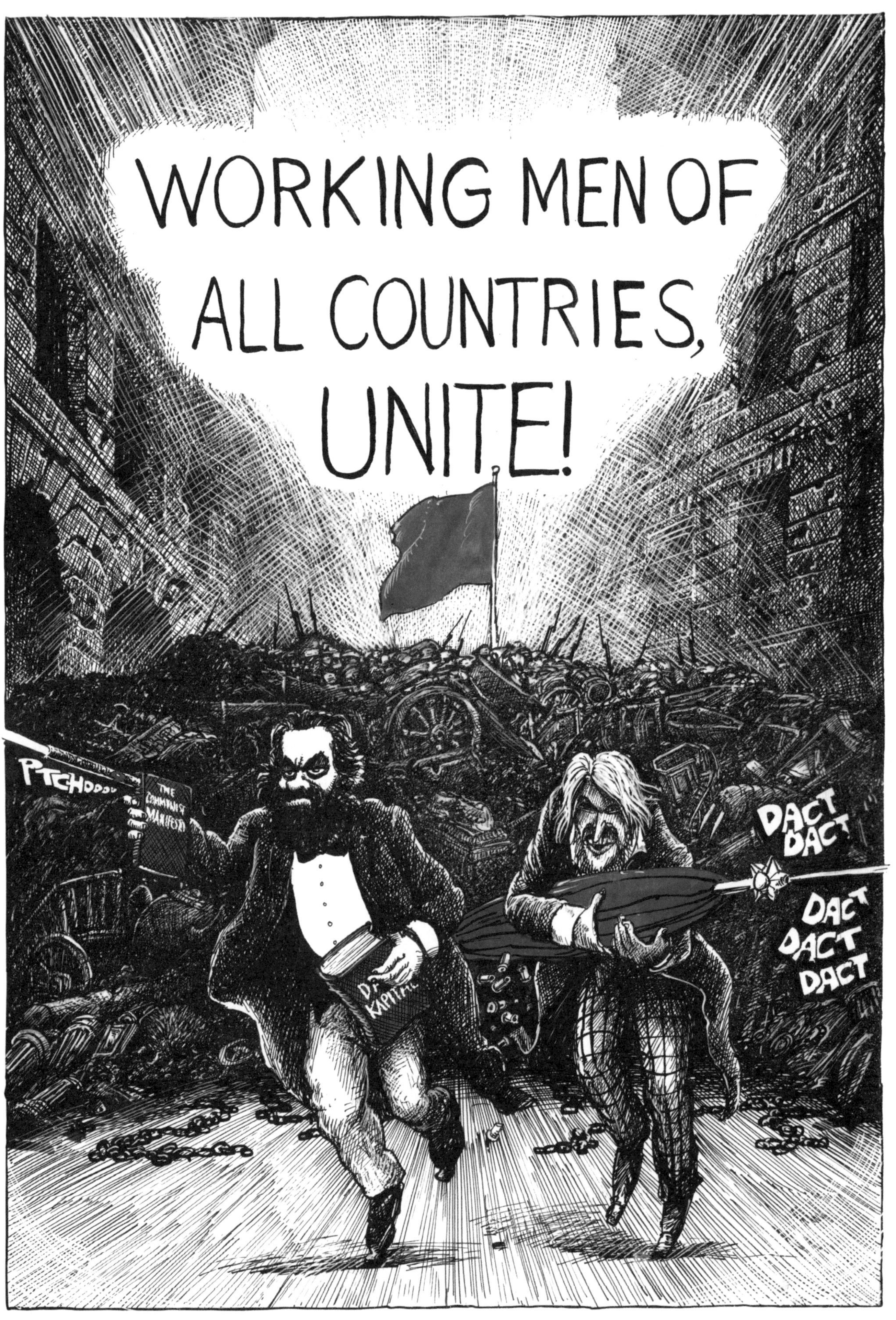

WORKING MEN OF ALL COUNTRIES, UNITE!
PTCHOOOO
THE COMMUNIST MANIFESTO
DACT DACT
DACT DACT DACT

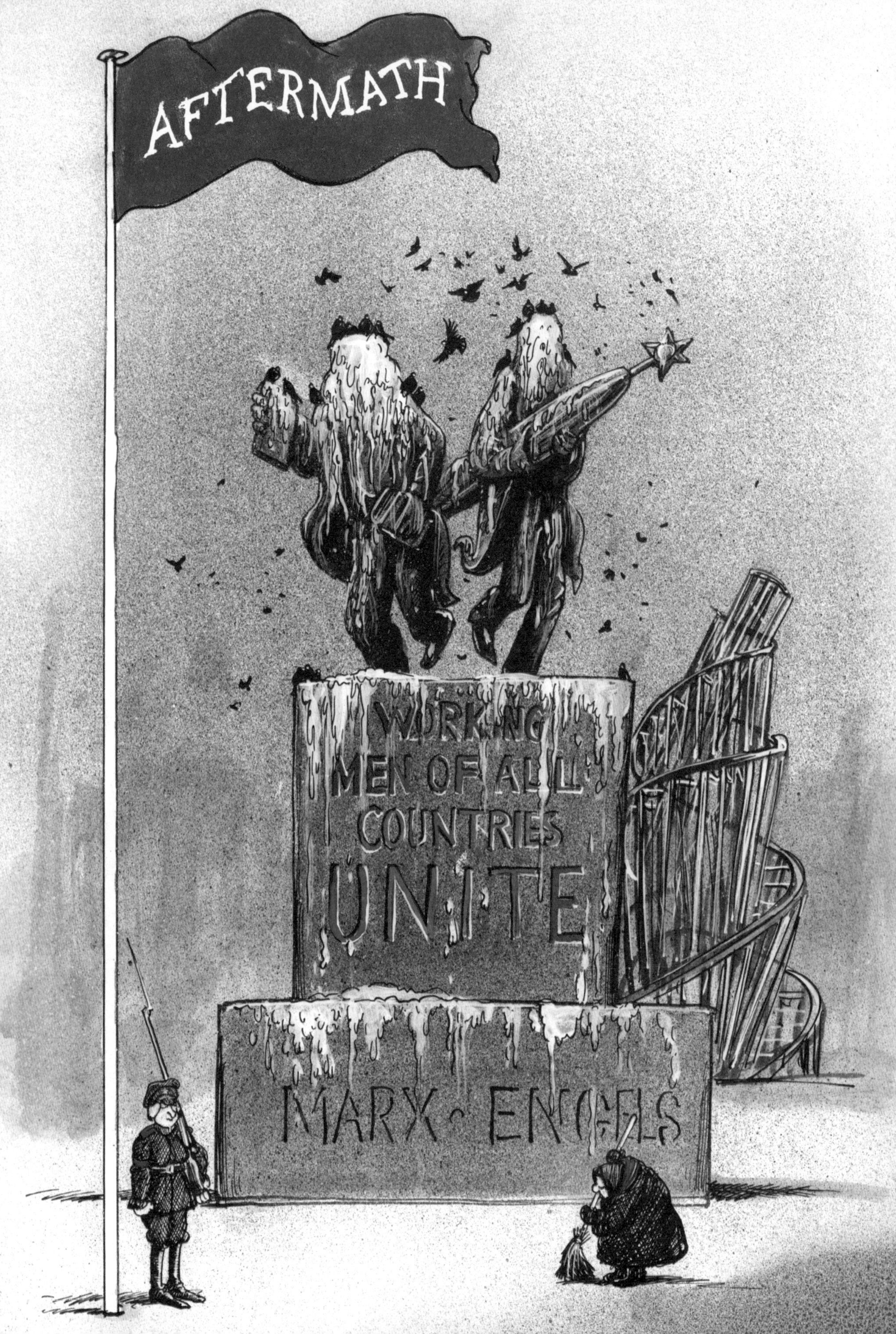
AFTERMATH
WORKING
MEN OF ALL
COUNTRIES
UNITE
MARX · ENGELS

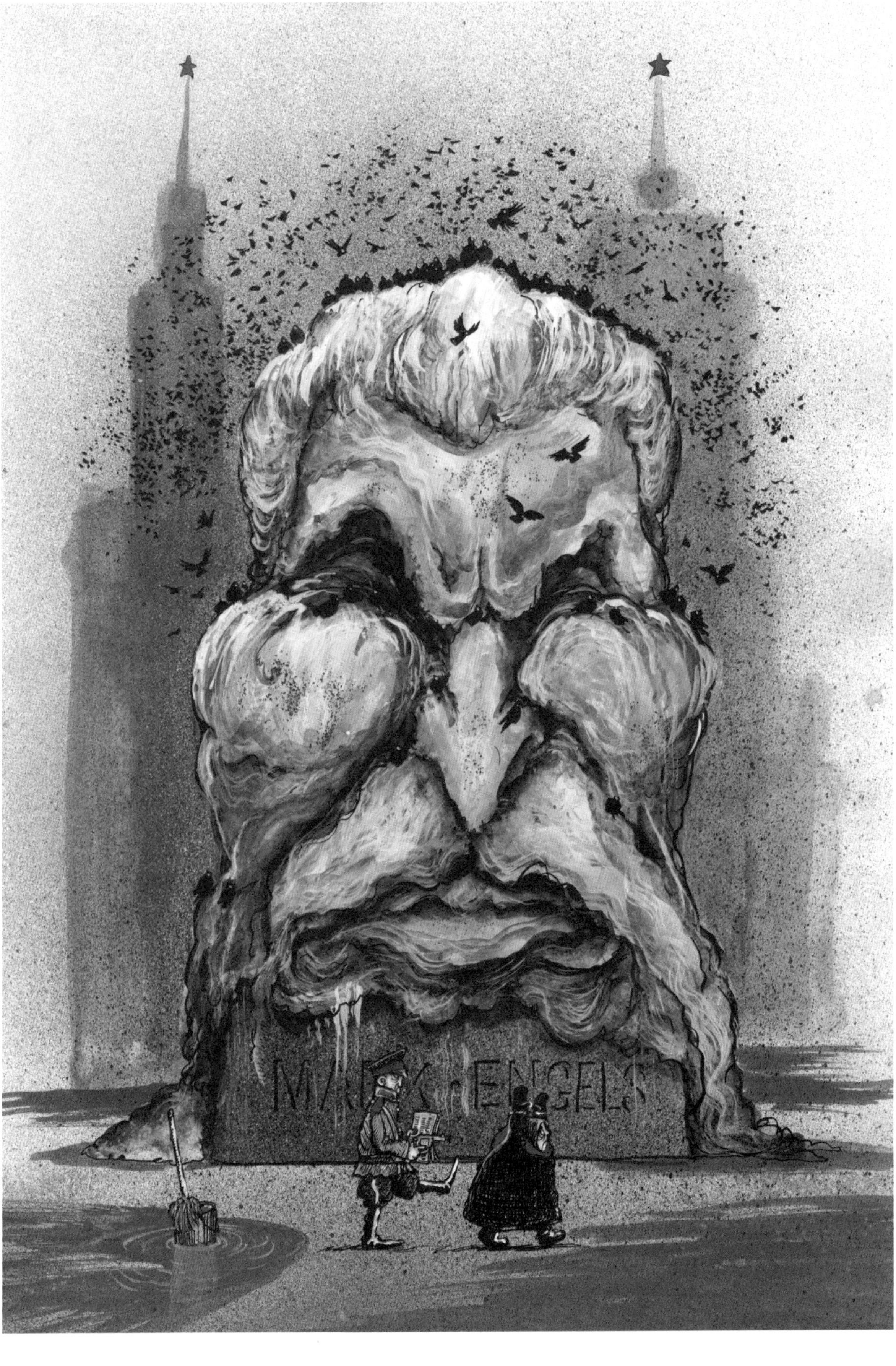

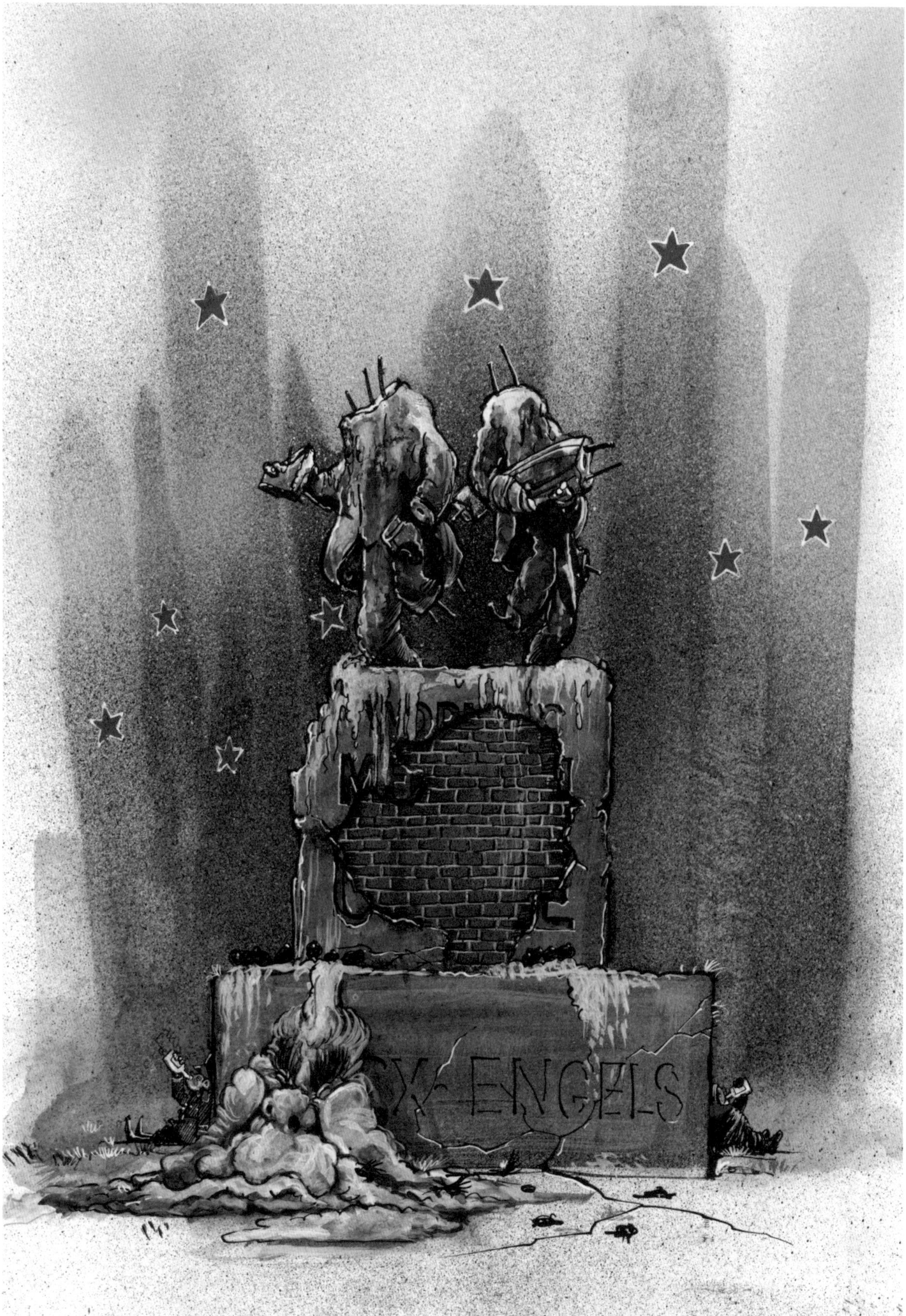
ENGELS

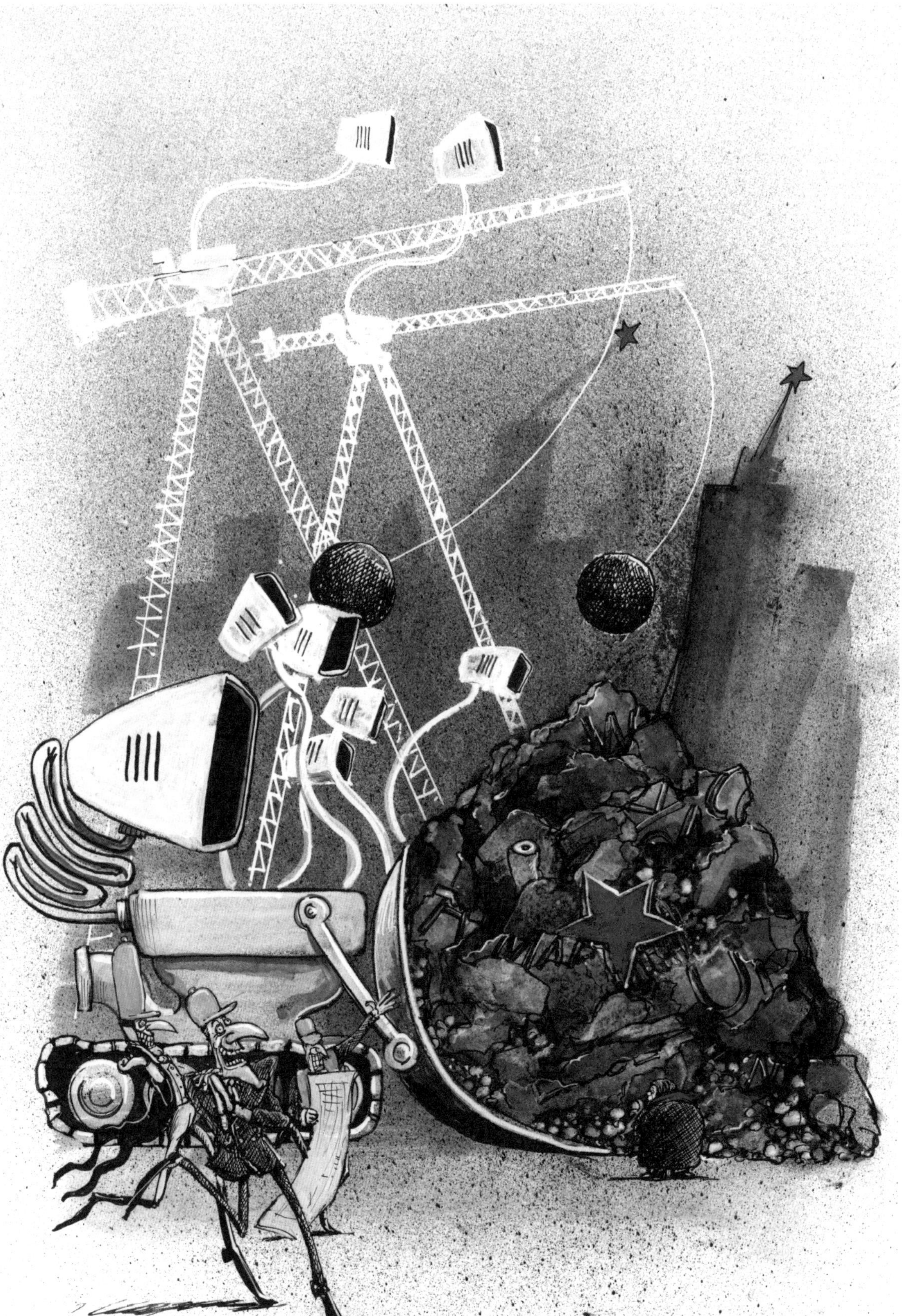

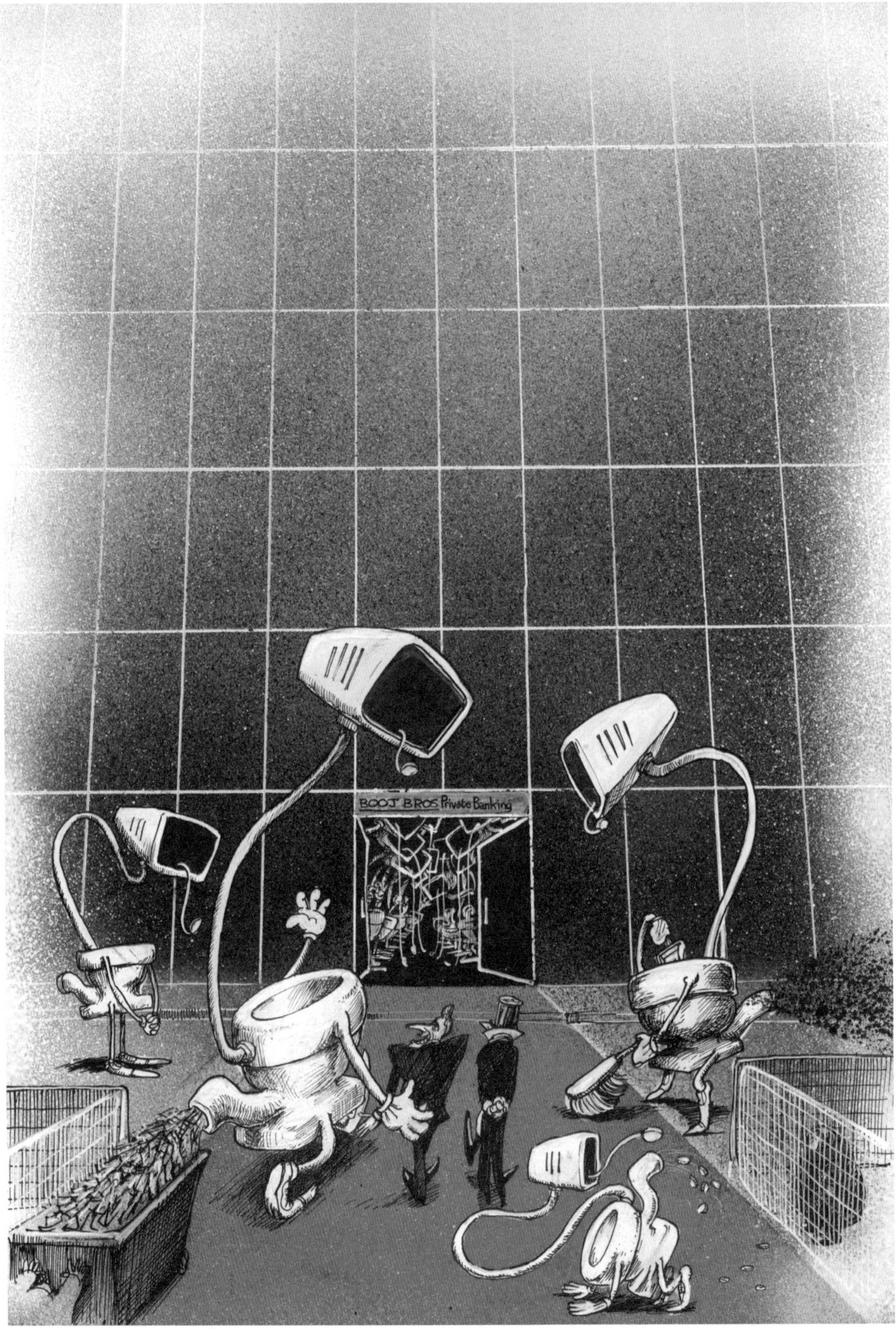
BOOJ BROS Private Banking

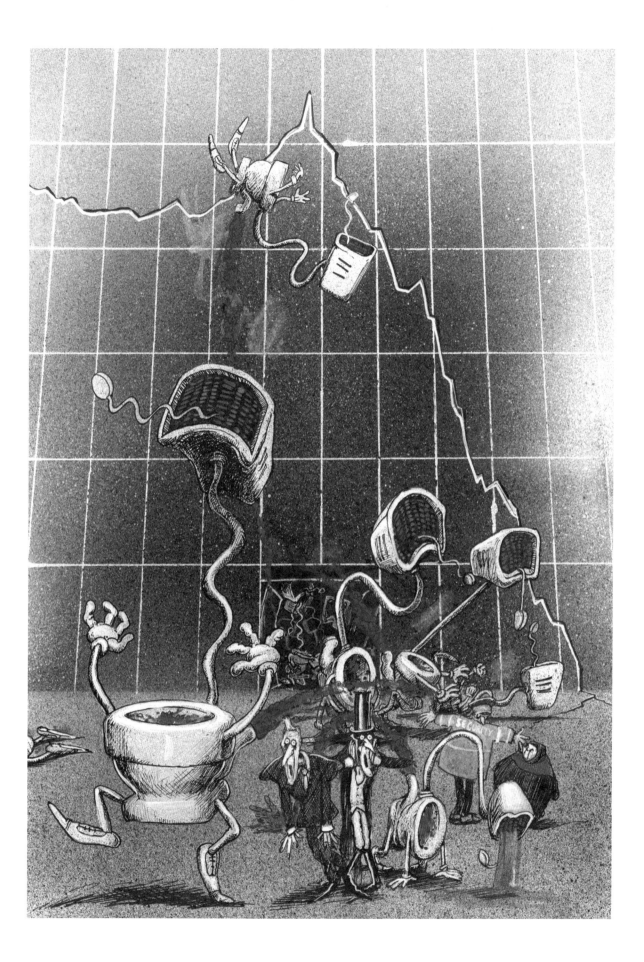

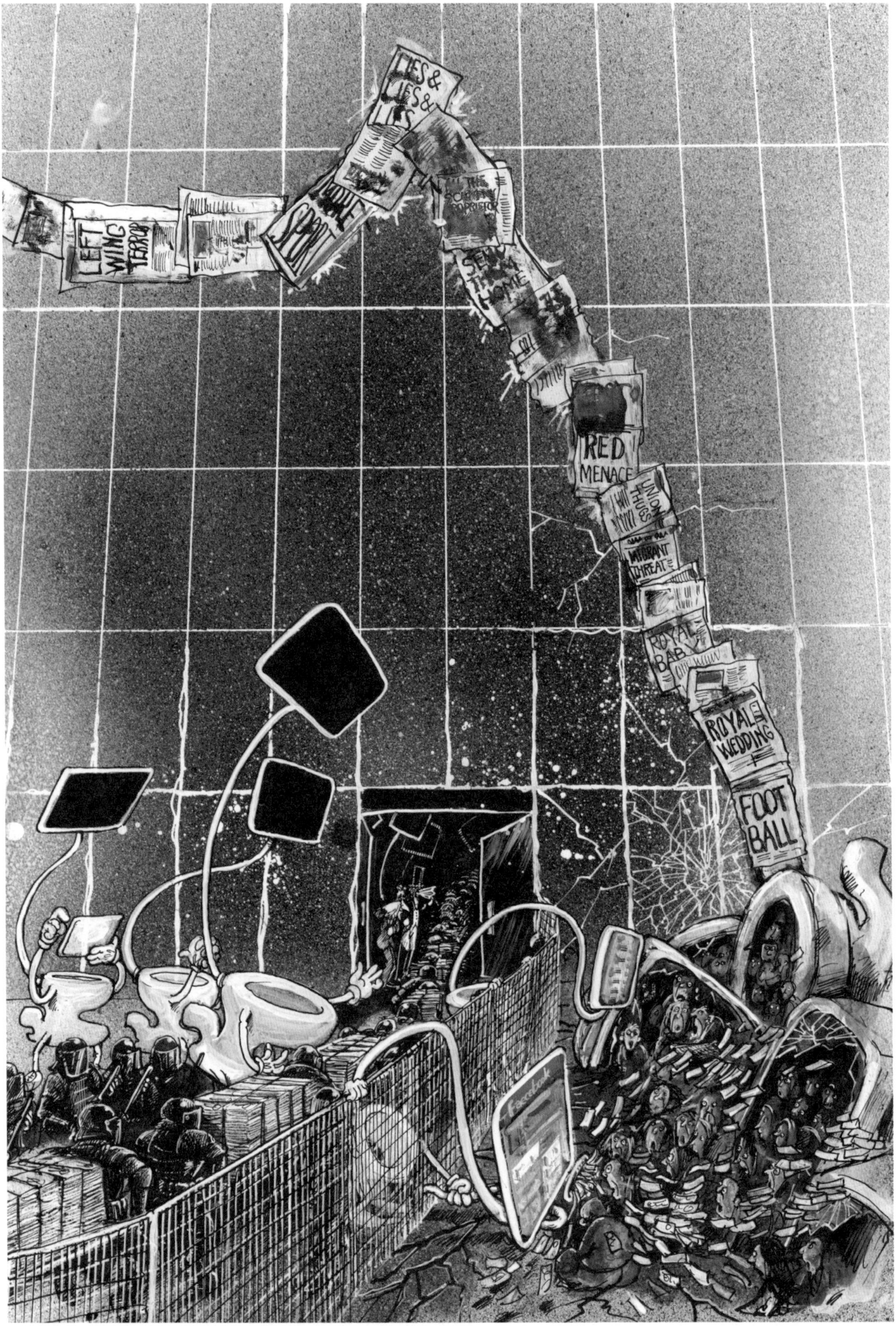
LEFT WING TERROR
RED MENACE
UNION THUGS
MIGRANT THREAT
ROYAL BABY
ROYAL WEDDING
FOOT BALL

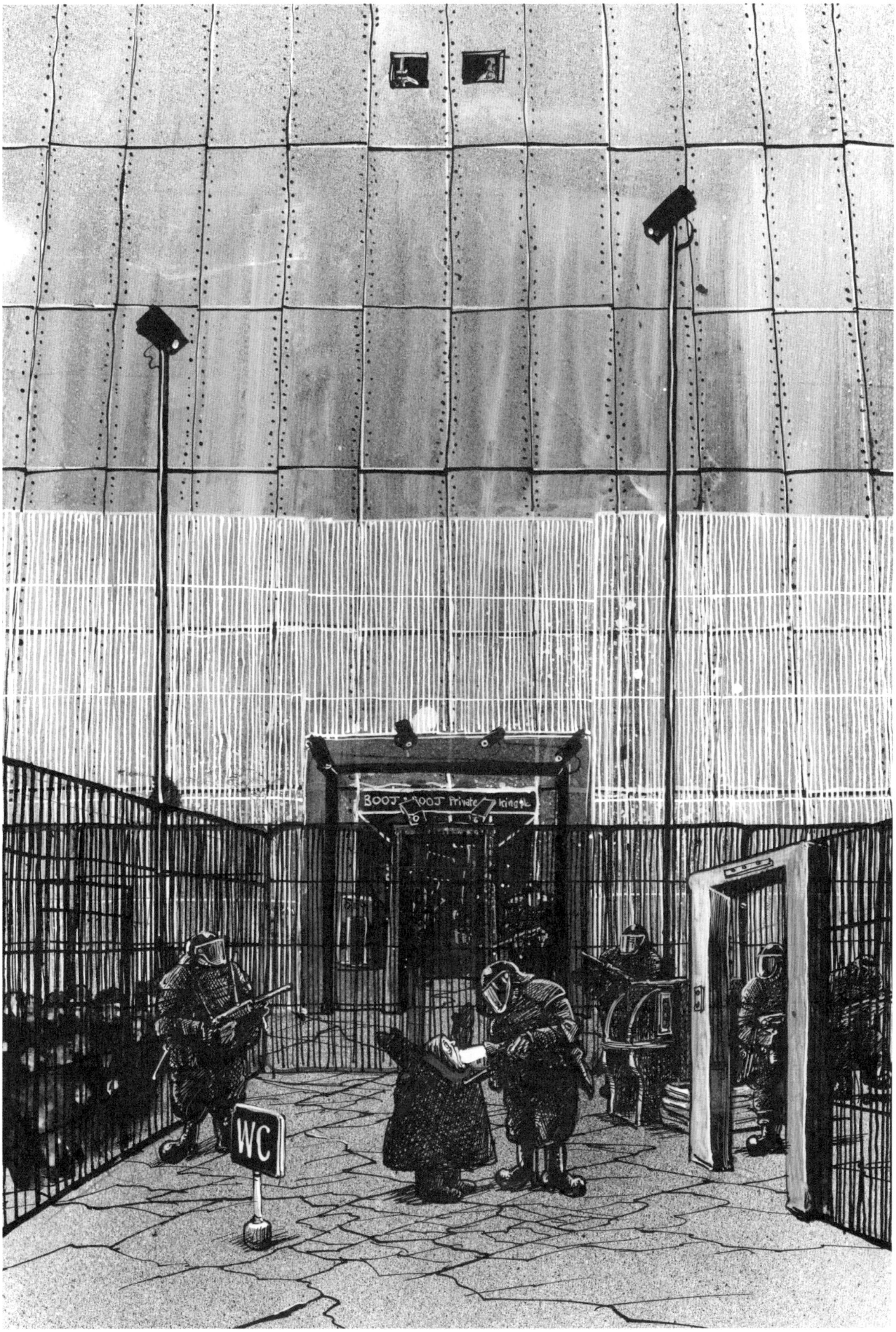
BOOJ
Private
WC

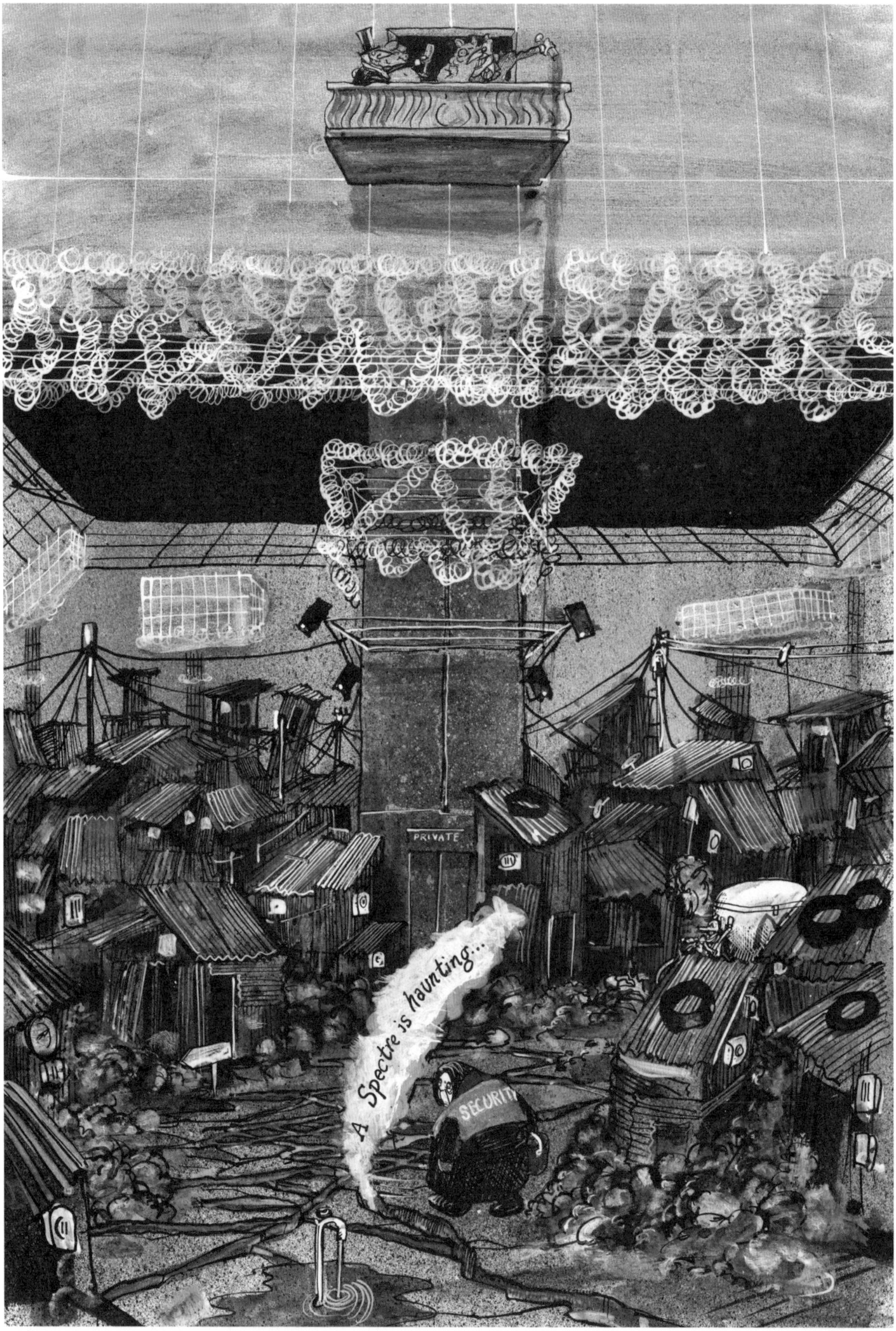
PRIVATE
A Spectre is haunting...
SECURITY

ACKNOWLEDGEMENTS

I want to thank Emma Hayley, Guillaume Rater and everyone else at SelfMadeHero, who are, as ever, a joy and pleasure to work with; my agent Sam Copeland and his colleagues at Rogers, Coleridge and White, for looking after the workers' interests (i.e. mine); my wife Anna Clarke for her wisdom and guidance in showing me the way forward when some of Marx's philosophical paradoxes, after the 50th re-reading, left me utterly baffled; the great Ralph Steadman, who initially schooled me in the use of the mouth atomiser, without which this book would have taken ten times as long to draw; whatever the collective noun is for the collection of historians and scholars into whose work I plunged in preparation; and finally, I want to thank my unwitting collaborators Karl Marx and Friedrich Engels, whose company I've genuinely enjoyed.

ABOUT MARTIN ROWSON

Martin Rowson is a multi-award-winning cartoonist, illustrator and writer whose work over the past three decades has appeared regularly in the *Guardian*, the *Daily Mirror*, *The Times*, the *Spectator*, the *Morning Star* and almost every other publication you can think of apart from *The Sun*, but only because they never asked him. His books include comic book adaptations of T.S. Eliot's *The Waste Land*, Laurence Sterne's *Tristram Shandy* and Jonathan Swift's *Gulliver's Travels*, as well as *Stuff*, a memoir about clearing out his late parents' house, which was long-listed for the 2006 Samuel Johnson Prize. Rowson is chair of the British Cartoonists' Association and is currently serving his third term as a vice-president of the Zoological Society of London. In 2017, one of his *Guardian* cartoons provoked a full-page editorial in the *Daily Mail*, which described him and his work as "disgusting... deranged... sick and offensive".

Martin Rowson lives in South London with his wife. Their son and daughter drop by now and then.

The Communist Manifesto is free from copyright. The reference text used for this adaptation is the 1888 edition, translated by Samuel Moore and approved by Friedrich Engels.

First published in 2018
by SelfMadeHero
139-141 Pancras Road
London NW1 1UN
www.selfmadehero.com

Written by Karl Marx and Friedrich Engels
Adapted by Martin Rowson

Publishing Director: Emma Hayley
Sales & Marketing Manager: Sam Humphrey
Editorial & Production Manager: Guillaume Rater
UK Publicist: Paul Smith
US Publicist: Maya Bradford
Designer: Txabi Jones
With thanks to: Dan Lockwood and Nick de Somogyi

A CIP record for this book is available from the British Library

ISBN: 978-1-910593-49-3

10 9 8 7 6 5 4 3 2 1

Printed and bound in Slovenia